365 Days of Taste-Berry™
Inspiration for Teens

365 Days of Taste-Berry™ Inspiration for Teens

**Bettie B. Youngs, Ph.D., Ed.D.
Jennifer Leigh Youngs**
Authors of the bestselling
Taste Berries™ for Teens series

Health Communications, Inc.
Deerfield Beach, Florida

www.hci-online.com
www.tasteberriesforteens.com

Library of Congress Cataloging-in-Publication Data

365 days of taste-berry inspiration for teens / [compiled by] Bettie B. Youngs,
Jennifer Leigh Youngs ; with contributions from teens for teens.
   p. cm.
   ISBN 0-7573-0096-0
   1. Teenagers—Conduct of life—Miscellanea. I. Title: Three hundred and
sixty five days of taste-berry inspiration for teens. II. Youngs, Bettie B.
III. Youngs, Jennifer Leigh, date.

BJ1661 .A15 2003
158.1'28—dc21

                                                              2002038778

Publisher: Health Communications, Inc.
          3201 S.W. 15th Street
          Deerfield Beach, FL 33442-8190

Cover illustration and design by Andrea Perrine Brower
Inside book formatting by Dawn Von Strolley Grove

To: _____

. . . a taste berry 365 days a year!

From: _____

Also by Bettie B. Youngs, Ph.D., Ed.D.

A Teen's Guide to Christian Living (Health Communications, Inc.)

A Teen's Guide to Living Drug-Free (Health Communications, Inc.)

A Taste-Berry Teen's Guide to Setting & Achieving Goals (Health Communications, Inc.)

Taste Berries for Teens #3: Inspirational Stories and Encouragement on Life, Love, Friends and the Face in the Mirror (Health Communications, Inc.)

A Taste-Berry Teen's Guide to Managing the Stress and Pressures of Life (Health Communications, Inc.)

More Taste Berries for Teens: A Second Collection of Inspirational Short Stories and Encouragement on Life, Love, Friendship and Tough Issues (Health Communications, Inc.)

Taste Berries for Teens Journal: My Thoughts on Life, Love and Making a Difference (Health Communications, Inc.)

Taste Berries for Teens: Inspirational Short Stories and Encouragement on Life, Love, Friendship and Tough Issues (Health Communications, Inc.)

Taste-Berry Tales: Stories to Lift the Spirit, Fill the Heart and Feed the Soul (Health Communications, Inc.)

A String of Pearls: Inspirational Stories Celebrating the Resiliency of the Human Spirit (Adams Media)

Gifts of the Heart: Stories That Celebrate Life's Defining Moments (Health Communications, Inc.)

Values from the Heartland: Stories of an American Farmgirl (Health Communications, Inc.)

Stress & Your Child: Helping Kids Cope with the Strains & Pressures of Life (Random House)

You and Self-Esteem: A Book for Young People—Grades 5–12 (Jalmar Press)

Safeguarding Your Teenager from the Dragons of Life: A Parent's Guide to the Adolescent Years (Health Communications, Inc.)

How to Develop Self-Esteem in Your Child: 6 Vital Ingredients (Macmillan/Ballantine)

Self-Esteem for Educators: It's Job Criteria #1 (Jalmar Press)

Helping Your Child Succeed in School (Active Parenting)

Developing Self-Esteem in Your Students: A K–12 Curriculum (Jalmar Press)

Getting Back Together: Repairing the Love in Your Life (Adams Media)

Is Your Net-Working? A Complete Guide to Building Contacts and Career Visibility (John Wiley)

Managing Your Response to Stress: A Guide for Administrators (Jalmar Press)

Stress Management Skills for Educators (Jalmar Press)

Problem Solving Skills for Children (Jalmar Press)

Also by Jennifer Leigh Youngs

Feeling Great, Looking Hot & Loving Yourself! Health, Fitness and Beauty for Teens (Health Communications, Inc.)

A Teen's Guide to Christian Living (Health Communications, Inc.)

A Teen's Guide to Living Drug-Free (Health Communications, Inc.)

A Taste-Berry Teen's Guide to Setting & Achieving Goals (Health Communications, Inc.)

Taste Berries for Teens #3: Inspirational Stories and Encouragement on Life, Love, Friends and the Face in the Mirror (Health Communications, Inc.)

A Taste-Berry Teen's Guide to Managing the Stress and Pressures of Life (Health Communications, Inc.)

More Taste Berries for Teens: A Second Collection of Inspirational Short Stories and Encouragement on Life, Love, Friendship and Tough Issues (Health Communications, Inc.)

Taste Berries for Teens Journal: My Thoughts on Life, Love and Making a Difference (Health Communications, Inc.)

Taste Berries for Teens: Inspirational Short Stories and Encouragement on Life, Love, Friendship and Tough Issues (Health Communications, Inc.)

Acknowledgments

We would like to thank the "taste berries" in the development of this book. First, to the many teens who were a part of the many books in our *Taste Berries for Teens* series: Thank you for so generously sharing your experiences so that other teens might better understand theirs. As always, you teach us the importance of living close to your heart and to greet each day with anticipated wonder. A very special thanks to the parents, educators, school administrators and counselors who support teens in bringing the words of their experiences to us. We are so appreciative.

As always, we extend a heartfelt gratitude to our publisher, Peter Vegso, whose vision of "changing the world one book at a time" is an awesome model of bringing all that is noble about being a taste berry into the world. We'd also like to thank the staff at Health Communications—most especially those with whom we work most closely: Susan Tobias, Lisa Drucker, Christine Belleris, Lori Golden, Kim Weiss, Randee Feldman, Tom Sand, Larissa Henoch, Elisabeth Rinaldi, Andrea Perrine Brower and Terry Burke, as well as to so many others who are intricately woven into transporting our works into the hands and hearts of our readers.

We also extend a very special thanks to the taste berries in our office who worked closely on this project—most especially Tina Moreno and a staff of teens whose valuable input in this book is evident throughout. Most importantly, we give glory to God, from whom all blessings flow.

Bettie and Jennifer Youngs

Introduction

Dear Teens,

Welcome to *365 Days of Taste-Berry Inspiration for Teens,* a book intended for exactly what the title prescribes: 365 vignettes of inspiration you can use on a daily basis. We wrote this book because we receive so many letters from teens telling us how a passage from one of the books in our *Taste Berries for Teens* series has brought them valuable insight or inspiration, and encouraged or influenced them—or a friend—to act in taste-berry ways. So here is your book of taste berries—one for each day of the year!

Affirmations (or "affies" as so many of you fondly refer to them!) serve a powerful purpose in our lives: They encourage us to remember—in the good times, and most especially in the tough times—all that is sweet and lasting in life. These blessings include the nature and quality of our lives, the people we love and care about and the values for which we stand. Just as the taste berry (the metaphor we use in the *Taste Berries for Teens* series) transforms even bitter bites into sweet ones, affirmations can sweeten your experience of life. Affirmation, by its very definition, means *affirming or saying yes to the truth.* Because an affirmation is a reminder of the truths you aspire to in your heart and soul, it supports you in your goal to keep reaching toward your personal best. Snippets of truth and wisdom, part of the power of affirmations, are found in the fact that they act as "sweeteners" when you're going through a confusing or difficult time, or have a stressful day ahead of you. There are times when we could all use inspiration and encouragement, whether to boost our confidence, restore hope or simply to remind us to choose the "high road."

Uplifting, loving, motivating and completely practical, the "taste-berry thoughts" we've provided in this volume are sure to remind you of your highest ideals and inspire you to continue claiming them as your own. The passages we've chosen to include in this book are those that remind you of the power of love, friendship, integrity, compassion, kindness, service, forgiveness, taking action, courage, perseverance and the many other taste-berry traits and qualities that call you to live a life of meaning, purpose and success. Our hope is that you find joy and motivation in each day as you take these precious reminders to heart.

As you'll see, each day's reading opens with one of your favorite quotes from the *Taste Berries for Teens* series. (The book is noted so that you can go back and read more from it if you choose!) The quote is then followed by encouraging and illuminating thoughts-for-the-day that are aimed to help you reflect on the meaning of the quote and to own it more deeply. At the end of each page, you'll find a "Taste-Berry Promise for the Day"— which is a terrific way to turn the affirmation into a commitment to live it as you face your travels through teen life. And it's a busy life, filled with activities—such as social commitments, special relationships, homework, sports, chores at home—which is another reason why it's so important to take the time to feed your heart and soul. We suggest you take a few minutes each morning to read the taste-berry inspiration for the day, reflecting on it and how to integrate it into your life, and then owning its promise. You may even want to take a minute each night to review your day, contemplating how and when you applied the inspiration, as well as how you might always make it a part of daily life. Since each day is numbered 1 through 365, you can begin at any time of the year (and you won't miss out on a "taste-berry inspiration" if, for some reason, you have to skip a day's reading).

As always, we'd like to hear from you. Please tell us how this book of daily inspirations made a difference to you—and to those with whom you share your daily life. To contact us:

Taste Berries for Teens
3060 Racetrack View Drive
Del Mar, CA 92014
or, *www.tasteberriesforteens.com*

Taste Berries to You!
Bettie and Jennifer Youngs

Be a Taste Berry!

When we help others by sweetening life's joys and easing the bitterness of its disappointments and losses—by helping them see our world as full of hope, less impossible and more glorious—we become their taste berry.

Bettie B. Youngs
Taste Berries for Teens

The *richardella-dulcisica*—or the "taste berry" as it is commonly and affectionately called—is a magical little red berry that mysteriously convinces our taste buds to experience all foods—even bitter bites—as sweet and delicious. *People* can—and must—be "taste berries" to each other. Make it your honor—as much as your obligation—to help, support and encourage others. Doing this can sweeten the experience of their journey. And bring meaning and purpose to yours.

Taste-berry promise for the day: I will write it upon my heart to be a taste berry to others.

Life Is Good: Be Grateful!

Especially when you're feeling bad or facing a tough time, remember all the ways your life is good.

Paige Williams, 17
More Taste Berries for Teens

Sometimes it's difficult to see the good in your life when you're overwhelmed by stress, struggling with a problem or have a broken heart. Especially at those times, recall what is good and positive in your life. Doing this helps you feel that in spite of a hardship you're facing, all in all, your life is good and you are thriving—and so you will vow to persevere through this challenge. You are grateful for all that is good, and so *hope* takes over. Hope makes it possible for your strength to be renewed, your stamina to be restored and your spirit to be lifted. And here's even better news: Gratitude is an attitude! And so, the "remote" to tune it in and turn it up a notch is in YOUR hands. Make it your desire to be grateful, and all else will seem possible.

Taste-berry promise for the day: I will tell my best friend three things for which I am grateful.

Day 3

You Are the Best You

You are you—and that is who you are supposed to be.

Bettie B. Youngs
Taste Berries for Teens

There is only one of you. No one else in the world shares your fingerprints. No one else can experience the way your heart feels about things. No one can see through the lens you use to see life quite the same as you do. Be in *awe* of this individuality—but *accept* it, too. *Honor* it. *Praise* it. Do not be quick to compromise it. In your desire to fit in or make others happy, you may be tempted to pretend to be someone you are not. You may even pretend to believe things you don't really believe, or act in ways that are out of character with who you really are. When you do this, you lose out on the real you. As importantly, the world loses out on you, too. Strive to be a healthy, happy and enlightened person—and then, taking your place alongside your fellow travelers, offer this self to the waiting world.

Taste-berry promise for the day: I will be *me*—because it is the most distinctive contribution I can offer.

Care for Yourself

Caring for yourself—mind, body and soul—is the most important job you'll ever have.

Jennifer Leigh Youngs
Feeling Great, Looking Hot & Loving Yourself! Health, Fitness and Beauty for Teens

It's so easy to get caught up in the whirlwind of activities in the exciting lives we each create for ourselves! And yet, aside from the activities we revolve around, and the people with whom our lives are intertwined, we must never forget to care for ourselves. Yes, we are strong, confident and resilient. Still, we are small and fragile and in need of care, as well. You know this of course; it's why you treat others gently, kindly and with respect for their well-being. You must do nothing less for yourself. Not only are good nutrition, rest and exercise essential to your health and wellness, they are also important "ingredients" in your ability to manage daily life. Also important is exercising the muscle of your mind and nourishing your spirit. Doing these things helps you be your best and do your best in all that you do. Take care of yourself: Don't mistreat yourself or put yourself at risk. Your body, mind and soul are yours to look after—be a taste berry: See that you do.

Taste-berry promise for the day: I will read a book that will help improve my life.

4

Seeing Yourself Through Others

Amazing, isn't it, how seeing one's own worth and beauty comes easier when you see it reflected in the stars in another's eyes.

Kayleigh Minutella, 14
More Taste Berries for Teens

When others see you as worthy, filled with the shining beauty of being a loveable person, the warm glow of their regard just lights up your own sense of self. Always in search of meaning, it's as though we first seek to define our worth from the outside in. When others find us worthy, we then give ourselves permission to believe in our worth, as well. There is a positive outcome to all this: Feeling admired and loved affirms that you are a loving person. Being a loving person confirms that you can love and admire others. What good news: The sincere admiration of others encourages and inspires us to know love. This is another reason to be taste berries to one another: We help each other expand our capacity to love and be loved.

Taste-berry promise for the day: I will see the stars in my own eyes.

You Can Change the World

Do good works, even when no one will know that you've contributed. It might change someone else's life—maybe even your own. It may even change the world.

Erin Bishop, 17
Taste Berries for Teens

We are all connected to one another, members of the same human family. Each of us has the potential to uplift the other. Even small acts, like a pebble dropped in a pond, can create ripples of good. Know that your smile or kindness can inspire the person you were kind to, and he or she may then smile or be kind to someone else, who is then inspired to be kind and smile at someone else—creating waves of kindness in the world. Such is the way you can *change* the world, and is the current on which change within yourself flows into being.

Taste-berry promise for the day: I will write an anonymous thank-you note to someone who is a kind person.

How Are You Special?

We are all "special." What makes us "unique" is finding out HOW we are special.

Bettie B. Youngs
More Taste Berries for Teens

Yes, of course we are ALL special: No other person is exactly like you. But so much more is asked of you than to simply know that you are special; you must find out *how* you are special. In the work of understanding your nature and personality, and in discovering and developing your talents and aptitudes, "exactly how you are special" is revealed. Find out how you are a "one-of-a-kind" in the entire world. Respond to the *calling* within, beckoning you to embrace this truth.

Taste-berry promise for the day: I will look closely at HOW I am special, a "one-of-a-kind" in all the world.

7

Patience Is a Virtue

I am learning to be more patient than is my nature.

Bettie B. Youngs
Taste Berries for Teens #3

We live in a swift-paced, quick-fix, fast-food, instant-message society. Waiting is not something we like to do: We want immediate gratification. But "quick" and "instant" aren't necessarily best or blessed. Some things are better learned, processed or revealed through a more graceful pace of time—such as the healing of grief, the unfolding of dreams, meaningful reflection and abiding love. Patience is a sterling virtue precisely because it is the pace in which time-honored truths—even miracles—unfold for you. Learn to be patient—and wonder, joy and a loving nature will be yours.

Taste-berry promise for the day: I will practice patience with others and myself.

Love Makes the World Go 'Round

Love is the greatest "taste berry" of all.

Bettie B. Youngs
Taste Berries for Teens

Love—such a simple one-syllable word, and yet, perhaps the most profound word of all! Certainly love is important to our lives: It's been said that we *need* love in order to be healthy and happy. Being loved affirms that we are loveable, worth loving. It is also empowering: Knowing that we are loved makes *everything* seem possible! Yet, just as getting love—being *loved*—is a necessary element in our lives, so is the giving of it. Giving love validates that we are wanted and needed, and so it gives our lives great purpose. What a comforting thought: Love is all encompassing—and all nourishing. Take time each day to reflect on the ways that you are rising to the challenge of being a loving person. Notice how this improves your life—and the lives of those with whom you share it.

Taste-berry promise for the day: I will be more aware of how I am able to give and receive love.

Choose Happiness

You can choose happiness; you don't have to wait for it to come knocking at your door.

Jennifer Leigh Youngs
Feeling Great, Looking Hot & Loving Yourself! Health, Fitness and Beauty for Teens

Most anyone can tell you that being in the presence of someone who radiates sunshine is a most pleasant experience! But seeing the cup "half-full" rather than "half-empty" is more than a lovely addition to your persona. Being a happy person is also a benefit to your physical health and to your emotional wellness. Even better news is the fact that you can *choose* to be happy. You choose happiness by being a positive person and by seeing your life, and the world around you, as brightly as you can. You elect to see what is positive and good, rather than to dwell on the downside of things. As a result, your taste-berry approach is the instant sweetener in the adage, "When life deals you lemons, make lemonade." Be a happy person: Choose it.

Taste-berry promise for the day: I will choose to be a happy person.

10

Have a Plan

This next year, I'm going to do things a lot different than I did last year. I know I said this last year, but I am absolutely positively sure I'm changing my ways this next school year!

Cammie Brinthall, 15
A Taste-Berry Teen's Guide to Setting & Achieving Goals

Do you start out with great intentions, but then get sidetracked from accomplishing the things you want to get done? It can happen—especially if you haven't yet turned your hopes, dreams and desires into concrete plans. When you have a plan for achieving the things you want to accomplish, things aren't left to chance. A plan points you in the direction of what you should be doing each month, week and day to move closer to your goals. In short, you know where to focus your time and energy. Channeling your efforts in a specific direction can keep you on track to getting what you want, to bringing your intentions to fruition. What are three things you can do today to move you closer to achieving your goals? Be sure to put your answers and your goals in writing. This helps you "see" the plan!

Taste-berry promise for the day: I will create a reminder of my goals to keep me focused on achieving them and post it where I will see it often.

Appreciate Your Parents' Love

It was a very beautiful moment, a real expression of their love—my parents, dancing together in the kitchen!

Cory Griffin, 17
Taste Berries for Teens

It can be easy to overlook the fact that your parents may have the same young heart for love as you do. Love is like that: It transcends time; it never "gets old." Embrace the love your parents have for one another! Let them know how refreshing it is to "see" their love. Tell them how "safe" it makes you feel when they demonstrate their love. Even if your parents are separated or no longer together, you can appreciate the love they once shared—being grateful your life was created by that love.

Taste-berry promise for the day: I will tell my parents that I am thankful for their having loved one another enough to bring me into the world.

Part of a Greater Whole

Eavesdrop on the still, quiet way the universe unites you to all life.

Jennifer Leigh Youngs
Feeling Great, Looking Hot & Loving Yourself! Health, Fitness and Beauty for Teens

You've felt a tug inside your heart to offer kind eyes and a smile to a stranger in passing. You've felt compelled to softly stroke and speak gently to an animal. You've felt a sense of completeness when you see a couple walking hand-in-hand. You've felt the twinge of your own goodness when you encouraged or helped someone out in a moment of need. Contemplate how this is the evidence of the mysterious unity that exists in being part of a much greater whole. If this were not so, would you feel these sacred nudges, hear these whispers of grace or even care about their calls? Accept what you feel. Such "stirrings" are proof positive of the power of connection—and the importance of you having connected.

Taste-berry promise for the day: I will remember that I am part of a much greater whole.

You Get What You Give

*T*hink *"boomerang"! What you send out comes back!*

Becky Coldwell, 15
Taste Berries for Teens Journal

If you treat people with kindness, usually you'll find that people treat you with kindness in return. If you are giving and attentive, people respond to you in the same way. By the same token, when you are grouchy and impatient with others, you may get it back in return, as well! So what about those times when you were kind and the person didn't respond to you with kindness? It may feel like someone gobbled up your taste berry without even saying thanks. It can be comforting to think that all the positive energy and goodwill you send out in the world come back to you, but it may not always be so. Sometimes the boomerang that lands in your space belongs to someone else altogether. Likewise, sometimes your kindness actually boomerangs to another person entirely. Do not keep score: Your job is to tend to the boomerangs you send out.

Taste-berry promise for the day: I will say something encouraging to five people.

Shoot for Your Goals

ou always miss 100 percent of the shots you don't take!

Jennifer Leigh Youngs
A Taste-Berry Teen's Guide to Setting & Achieving Goals

In pursuing any goal, there's always the chance of not reaching it. But there's also the possibility of success. On the one hand, you can "play it safe"—and choose not to try at all. No chance of failure there—except that your self-image will suffer because it knows you're missing out on the thrill and satisfaction of living courageously. You can also play the game of life halfheartedly—plod along, making ordinary goals, never "going for it!" Or, you can press yourself to think bold and dream big, and encourage yourself to play vigorously and boldly shoot for your goals. Yes, you may miss a few, but you can't score if you don't take aim and shoot! So chance it: Dream a dream, make a plan and go for it.

Taste-berry promise for the day: I will take one specific action toward reaching a goal.

15

Promote World Peace

orld peace is about the words we use, our attitudes and the ways we're willing to help others feel a part of things. World peace is a heart goal.

Diana Seretis, 14
Taste Berries for Teens #3

Do you believe in world peace but wonder how to teach or promote it? You personally can promote peace by living with a caring attitude and actions of respect, kindness and tolerance. If someone accidentally bumps into you, you have a choice: You can glare at the person, or you can hold your impulse and instead allow for the fact that it was an accident and dismiss it. One response promotes peace, while the other promotes conflict. Each of us has a responsibility to do our part to promote peace. What you say and what you do matter: They can either add to peace or take away from it. When you choose to live in peace, your words, actions and attitudes create peace. Listen to your heart and follow it: Strive toward *its* goal of peace.

Taste-berry promise for the day: I will be a peace-keeper and control impulses that do not promote peace.

Face Your Fears

The more of life I master, the less of life I fear.

Jennifer Leigh Youngs
Taste Berries for Teens

When faced with a new situation, and especially when confronting a challenge, it's normal to feel anxious—even fearful. Decide to confront it head-on. Just by taking action you'll find your fear subsiding. The reward is taste-berry sweet: Having proven to yourself that you can and will be proactive—take action—you'll have a new level of bravery. When you've faced your fears and been victorious, mastery is yours. This is the moment when you will learn the meaning of Sir Edmund Hillary's famous words: "It's not just the mountain we conquer but ourselves."

Taste-berry promise for the day: I will take action to get through a challenge, refusing to let fear stop me.

Life Is Sacred

When you look at our Earth home from space, you are filled with the belief that life is sacred. We must each care deeply.

Steve Smith, astronaut
Taste Berries for Teens

We can experience precious moments of connection to the vastness of creation when we take the time to stop and reflect. Perhaps you've looked at a star-dusted sky and thought about the infinite number of planets, or you've splashed in the ocean and thought of the never-ending waves and marveled at the mysterious and powerful pull of the tides. Maybe you've sat at the edge of a gaping canyon, or stared up at a forest of towering trees, or seen how a dried seed transforms into the most exquisite and intricate and colorful flower—and known a moment of absolute certainty that something far greater was at work in their creation. Allow this awe of creation to spark a deep reverence for the presence of the hand of the Creator. Being moved by this awe, you have an intuitive sense that you're called to care for all life as sacred. Surrender to the faith it commands.

Taste-berry promise for the day: I will pick up any litter I see in my neighborhood.

Be Good to Yourself

*ℒ ife is complicated for most everyone. We all experi-
ence that which pains us, that which annoys us, that
which challenges us. We must each take care of ourselves in
such times.*

Jordanne Guy, 19
A Taste-Berry Teen's Guide to Managing the Stress and Pressures of Life

No one's life is without trial and tribulations. No one's life is
stress-free. While the goal is to be proactive so as to minimize
having to always live life under duress or on the edge of chaos,
we must make concessions for when such times set in. During
those times when things are looking down and you're "stressed
to the max," be especially "extra-extra" good to yourself by rest-
ing and eating properly, and by releasing tension through exercise and relaxation. Be patient with yourself. Talk with others
about what's troubling you; getting something out in the open
diffuses its power over you. Make a list of all that is good in your
life. Allow your faith to comfort you. Don't *ever* forget to be a
taste berry to yourself.

Taste-berry promise for the day: I will go on a long,
relaxing walk.

Be Your #1 Fan

I keep my paintbrush with me,
wherever I may go,
in case I need to cover up,
so the real me doesn't show . . .

Lee Ezell
Taste Berries for Teens

Sometimes we think that in order to win favor and friendship from a particular person (or group), we have to "play into" that person, or we may even portray an image we think that person holds of us. Don't wear this "coat of paint." Putting on false airs or compromising who you are—trying to be someone you are not—is not a "color" you wish to become. Being "someone else" comes at the loss of your own self-respect. The desire to have others accept and like you is normal, even healthy. But even if they don't, you must always be your #1 fan. Be true to yourself. Make your goal self-acceptance. One taste berry in doing so is this: When you accept yourself, then others will, too.

Taste-berry promise for the day: I will feel good about myself and be "who I am" in all that I say and do.

Gossip Is Damaging

aking sure we don't "vandalize" others can be a real "taste berry"—to them as well as to ourselves.

Mia Templett, 14
Taste Berries for Teens

When you're with others who are talking about someone else, it can be easy enough to find yourself going along with the gossip. Throwing in your own "two cents" can make you feel like you fit in and have something of interest to share. The "boost" you feel at someone else's expense is never worth the damage done. When you move away from "taste-berry" actions, you forfeit your chance to help the world evolve into a better place. Be a part of that evolution: Choose to accentuate the positive and come to the aid of those being vandalized. Point out the person's positive qualities. Repaint the picture in a positive light.

Taste-berry promise for the day: I will not put myself down or do or say anything that could hurt anyone else.

Be Slow to Judge Others

Keep your own side of the street clean.

Jennifer Leigh Youngs
A Teen's Guide to Living Drug-Free

Sometimes we look at others through judgmental eyes: A person is "too cool" (or "not cool enough"), "too smart" (or "not smart enough"), or "too tall" (or "not tall enough"). When we pass judgment—when we're so worried about what others are doing on their "side of the street"—we ignore our own side of the street. But the truth is, the work of *self*-improvement is our only "road-crew" duty. Often, taking care of ourselves (and our own issues in life) is all the "street cleaning" we can handle. Make it your goal to be a healthy, happy and enlightened person. Do this and you will be "taste berry" enough.

Taste-berry promise for the day: I will look for my responsibility in situations and own my actions.

Be Honest About Your Feelings

Be honest—especially to yourself—about everything you are feeling.

Curt Lindholm, 15
Taste Berries for Teens

Sometimes it is difficult to admit to your feelings. Perhaps others are looking to you for leadership, and you are feeling inadequate. Maybe you feel as if you're supposed to be strong, so you can't let anyone know you feel insecure or vulnerable; or you're supposed to be brave, so you can't let anyone know you are scared. Sometimes it's even difficult to admit your feelings to yourself. Don't deny your feelings: Your feelings tell you just about everything you need to know about how you are faring in the world. They guide and direct you when you're off course, they signal when you need to take care of yourself, and they connect you to others who are wanting and willing to show you the way. They also allow you to rest when you need a reprieve from the world—or from yourself. Feelings are about seeing life through the eyes of your heart: Don't miss this view.

Taste-berry promise for the day: I will tell a parent or a friend something I feel insecure about.

Take the Time to Get to Know Someone

*M*ost of the time, people are more cool than you may think.

Carl Galloway, 14
Taste Berries for Teens

Sometimes first impressions are accurate. And, sometimes they are NOT. Often it takes time to get to know people to find out all the ways they are "totally cool." Spending time listening and sharing with a person can reveal that someone is kind, wise, funny, compassionate, loving, caring, brilliant, creative or simply "cool" in the best sense of the word. Broaden your horizons: Give the benefit of the doubt. Take the time to really get to know others. When you do, you're sure to find the world is full of taste-berry cool.

Taste-berry promise for the day: I will make time to get to know somebody new at school.

Your Opinion Matters Most

The opinion you have of yourself should not only count as much as anyone else's, but even more.

Jennifer Leigh Youngs
Taste Berries for Teens

All of us are vulnerable to the scrutiny of others; we want them to accept and approve of us. But what if they don't? It can hurt to be misunderstood, or to have someone judge you harshly or accuse you falsely. This might even work the other way around: Others may think you are bigger, better, brighter than you see yourself. Either way, it is your own opinion of yourself that matters the most. After all, you are the one person who you live with every day, the one person whose opinion you can never escape. Not only does this mean your opinion should count most, but it also means you are the one most qualified to have an opinion on the matter. Be a taste berry: Do those things to assure that your opinion of yourself is a positive one. In the least, be opinionated enough to have an opinion!

Taste-berry promise for the day: I will make my own little "bumper sticker" of inspiration that says, "I believe in me!" and put it where I can see it every day.

Everyone Needs Love

We live in a world that needs love.

Megan Haver, 16
More Taste Berries for Teens

It's been said that infants need love or they cannot survive. Children and adults need love to thrive. Like people, our world needs the essence of love to build a community of respect, fairness and concern for each other—no matter where we call "home." Creating a world filled with love begins with doing ordinary things each and every day: loving and caring for each of the members within our families, respecting the differences in our peers each day at school, and upholding the rules and laws of our communities in order to safeguard their citizens. It really is that simple, that "ordinary." The only part extraordinary about it is that you love yourself enough to do it.

Taste-berry promise for the day: I will put love and care into everything that I do.

Keep Your Promises

Keep the promises you make. It's how you learn to trust yourself.

Christopher Gillian, 17
A Teen's Guide to Living Drug-Free

If you make a promise, keep it. If you can't keep it, go tell the person you are not able to keep your promise and why. Your word means everything: It is an outward indicator of whether you are a person who has values like honesty and integrity, and an inner measure of your commitment to your "highest and best." Moreover, keeping your word is the single most important picture you will "snap" of yourself. Don't be caught having a "bad-hair" day. Make certain your picture reveals you in your best possible light—radiating integrity and traveling the "high road."

Taste-berry promise for the day: I will make good on all the promises I make.

Be with Positive People

$\mathcal{C}$hoose to be with those people who inspire and uplift you, and whose presence brings out your best.

Bettie B. Youngs
A Taste-Berry Teen's Guide to Setting & Achieving Goals

What really positive people do you know? Don't you find that you seem to do better in life when you are around them? Don't they make you feel more hopeful about yourself and life in general? Keeping company with those who inspire and uplift you helps you to do your best and be your best. When you're having a trying time, they're right there, absolutely believing that everything is going to turn out right. Choose friends who believe in you—those who motivate and support you. And be this kind of friend for others.

Taste-berry promise for the day: I will tell someone all the great things that are happening at our school.

Forgive Yourself—and Others

When you're able to forgive, you free yourself to live on a better, higher level.

Mikial Hirshorn, 16
More Taste Berries for Teens

Have you ever been forgiven for hurting someone you care about? Can you remember how it felt to be forgiven? Have you ever forgiven someone else for letting you down? The ability to ask for forgiveness is a strength born of trust. When you ask for forgiveness you trust in the other person's ability to exercise compassion; you trust that the other person's love is great enough to forgive. Sometimes it is easier to ask for the forgiveness of someone else than it is to forgive yourself—especially when you've hurt someone you love. If you're struggling with forgiving yourself, take a moment to tell yourself: "I forgive myself for forgetting who I truly am." Say this, trusting that your love is great enough to forgive. Most important, say it *knowing* that "who you truly are" is loving, caring and worthy of both giving and receiving forgiveness. Vow to reign on this "higher" level of living.

Taste-berry promise for the day: I will practice forgiving others as I wish to be forgiven.

Love What You Do

*T*he goal is to make your joys your job, your toys
your tools.

Jennifer Leigh Youngs
Taste Berries for Teens Journal

Have you ever met someone who absolutely loved his or her
work? If so, you probably also noticed that this person was
good-natured, joyous, energetic and happy to be of service to
you. It's like that when people love what they do. Don't miss the
opportunity to make "your joys your job"—to find what you
should do for work in life based around what will be joyous to
you. You don't have to look far; deep inside, you already know
what this is: You need merely to look to your interests, talents
and hobbies. What do you find interesting? What are your hobbies? What are your strengths? What are you doing when you
lose all sense of time? Chances are these are your innate abilities,
things that come easy and natural for you. Don't miss out! Doing
what you love is a big part of being happy in life. It's being who
you are and living a life that shows it.

Taste-berry promise for the day: I will think of three
jobs that would bring me joy.

Ask for Help

eaching out to others is a way to "double" our strength.

Bettie B. Youngs
A Teen's Guide to Living Drug-Free

A young boy and his father were out for a walk and came across a huge boulder on the road. The curious little boy looked up at his father and asked, "Dad, do you think I can move that big boulder?" His father looked at his son thoughtfully and then answered, "If you use all your strength, I know you can." So the little guy ran over, and straining and groaning, tried to move the huge rock, but of course, could not. Discouraged, he looked up at his father and said, "You're wrong, Dad. I can't do it." To this his father replied, "Oh, but you didn't use all your strength. You didn't ask me to help you." As the young boy discovered, you don't have to face obstacles alone. Often we make the assumption that we can do all things alone, when in reality our strength comes from reaching out. When you can use a helping hand to "lift" an obstacle out of your path, you "double your strength" by asking for help and assistance.

Taste-berry promise for the day: I will name those people who are there to help me when I need a hand.

Friends Show Their True Selves

> *When someone allows you to be vulnerable enough so as to reveal yourself—cracks, flaws and all—that person becomes really dear to you.*
>
> Jennifer Leigh Youngs
> *Taste Berries for Teens Journal*

When another person trusts you enough to totally be herself—holding back nothing, allowing you to glimpse that she is "all too human"—that person is paying you the highest compliment of all: *She trusts you.* That another person feels so safe about you as to reveal her innermost self—her hopes, dreams and aspirations, her deepest fears and darkest secrets—is a special responsibility. When someone has entrusted you to share in these personal and most sacred revelations, when she has honored you by disclosing these most private emotions, you must safeguard such information and, unless given permission, allow it to rest only within your own port. Knowing the value of such an entrusted friendship, seek out those who allow you such safe harbor, trusting that now you, too, can share your deepest truths and innermost self.

Taste-berry promise for the day: I will assure a friend that he or she can always share safely with me.

Stay Cool Under Pressure

*I*t's dumb to "freak-out" from stress: Instead, use it to fuel your doing something to get up and out of a stressful situation.

Janetta McGhee, 15
A Taste-Berry Teen's Guide to Managing the Stress and Pressures of Life

Your body is doing its remarkable work when it lets you know that it "feels" stress. Your job is to respond to the signals it's sending and convert this untamed energy to constructive and productive outcomes. Evaluate if the stress you're feeling is positive or negative. If stress motivates you to action, that's positive; if it stops you in its track or turns your "cool to ghoul," that's negative. There are lots of ways to stay cool under pressure, so learn all you can about how best to manage stress. The goal is to use stress to your advantage.

Taste-berry promise for the day: I will let my stress energize me to take action.

Identity Lies Within

The values of a person create the value in that person.

Bettie B. Youngs
Taste Berries for Teens

What are some of the things that you value about yourself? We can sometimes look for our "value" (or worth) external to ourselves, such as in the clothes we wear or in "who" our friends are. But looking outside of ourselves to find our worth will only provide a false sense of security: Styles change, and friends come and go. When we look outside of ourselves to define who we are or what we value, we come up wanting, because identity lies *within.* Are you looking for your worth? Search within.

Taste-berry promise for the day: I will list three values for which I stand.

Inspire Others

The next time you see someone you think is a "loser," reserve your cynicism. Instead, offer up a generous portion of encouragement. It may just be the ingredient that turns that person's life around.

Lisa Cartwright, 16
Taste Berries for Teens

There is enormous power in benevolence: When someone is down-and-out or having a tough day, rather than being critical, assume the role of a taste berry. The kindness of an outstretched hand can lift a person out of feelings of hopelessness, despair, anxiety and pain. As a result, this person will be better able to believe in his own abilities. Inspire such belief; it has the power to create great change. In what ways can you inspire others to believe in themselves?

Taste-berry promise for the day: I will tell a friend three reasons why I believe in him or her.

Day 36

Talk About Your Goals

Talking about your goals can help you discover what is really important to you—as well as what is not.

Jennifer Leigh Youngs
A Taste-Berry Teen's Guide to Setting & Achieving Goals

Clarifying what is important to you is a first step in laying claim to what you want out of life. A most excellent way to reach this point is to talk about your goals with your parents, friends and teachers—as well as with others who have your best interests at heart. Talking about your goals—and your plans for achieving them—allows you to "hear" yourself, which is an opportunity to see how strongly you (really) feel about things. And, of course, talking also allows you the benefit of hearing from others whose opinions you value. All can help you commit to certain goals and rethink others. Goals are about "being" and "becoming." Make sure you know where yours are leading!

Taste-berry promise for the day: I will talk with someone about my top three goals.

Show Compassion

Showing compassion is the mark of a taste berry.

Trisha Gerald, 18
More Taste Berries for Teens

How do you feel when you see a person crying, looking frightened or feeling bewildered? Have you been with a friend who was coming to grips with the realization that a special someone had betrayed her, or dealing with the heartbreak of learning that her parents were separating or getting divorced? Faced with another's pain, was there a stirring in your heart to offer compassion? Compassion is about understanding and empathy. It doesn't mean that you offer pity, nor sympathy, for that matter. It means you respect feelings, speak kindly and show support. Such "connection" allows others to feel less lonely and to know they are not traveling the journey alone. Someone else is there—and cares. And that someone is you.

Taste-berry promise for the day: I will ask a young child to tell me what he or she did today and listen carefully to the answer.

Set Your Boundaries

Setting boundaries is about knowing what you want and need, and then being willing to put a protective box around that.

Jennifer Leigh Youngs
Taste Berries for Teens #3

Boundaries define your standards. Others can readily "see" them. For example, if you're hanging around with a group of your friends, and someone in the group repeatedly uses "cuss" words and you find this offensive, would you say nothing, hoping that they would read your look of surprise, shock and disgust? Or would you simply say, "Please don't swear. It bothers me"? Or, "Do you really need to use all those adjectives?" Boundaries make things clear. Having boundaries not only shows another person what you find acceptable or not, but makes it clear that you are unwilling to compromise your high standards. Best of all, boundaries help you live your best and bring your best to others. How long does someone have to be with you before they can readily see your standards, your boundaries?

Taste-berry promise for the day: I will practice courage and set clear boundaries.

Families Are About Lasting Bonds

"*I love you because I know you so well; I love you in spite of knowing you so well!*"

Jennifer Leigh Youngs
Taste Berries for Teens

Often the very strongest bonds of love are those between parents and their children—and for good reason: Each of us sees the other at our best—and at our worst. We've been through each other's ups and downs together—and survived. Each knows the strengths and weaknesses of the other, and can even second-guess our moods! Thank goodness for families—we love each other, no matter what! Who do you love because you know that person so well—and love in spite of knowing so well? This person is most assuredly the sweetest of taste berries!

Taste-berry promise for the day: I will make a "Thanks for Being You" card for my parents.

Beauty Is More Than Outer Appearance

You carry your beauty with you every minute of every day, every place you go.

Jennifer Leigh Youngs
Feeling Great, Looking Hot & Loving Yourself! Health, Fitness and Beauty for Teens

Have you ever thought someone was beautiful and then, once you got to know that person, you decided he or she wasn't quite as beautiful as you'd once thought? Or perhaps you didn't consider someone as being beautiful until you started spending time with that person and then you thought he or she was one of the most beautiful people you'd ever met. It's like that, isn't it? So what makes someone beautiful? More than an outward glow, beauty is a character trait that radiates from within. Beauty shows up in the shine in your eyes and in a quick, genuine smile. It shows up in the way you carry yourself and in the ways in which you are benevolent to others. The good news is that anyone can be beautiful! Beauty, like happiness, is an attitude, which means it is chosen. Choose to be a beautiful person.

Taste-berry promise for the day: I will observe when and how I feel like a beautiful person.

Appreciate Someone

Letting someone know how much you appreciate something he's done for you is not only polite, but it also encourages that person to continue to do those kinds of things for others.

Ashley Lin, 12
Taste Berries for Teens #3

Do you know someone who always seems to be busy helping others? Can you think of somebody whose nature is consistently kind and caring? Do you have a friend or acquaintance who goes out of his or her way to be of service? When we see someone who is especially kind, or who spends his or her time and energy helping others, it's only natural to look at this person with admiration and respect. You appreciate her desire to help others and her genuine effort to be of service and to make the world a better place. Be sure to remind this person how cool you think it is that she exemplifies what it means to be a "taste berry." This kind of praise heartens others and can inspire them to continue to expand their efforts to make a difference in the world. And don't forget to take notes: You have met someone to emulate!

Taste-berry promise for the day: I will think of how I can honor someone in my community who is always kind.

Live in the Present

In the moment is the power of change, the path of good, the promise of hope. In the moment is where life is played out. It's all about living life—in present tense.

Bettie B. Youngs
A Teen's Guide to Living Drug-Free

Is there a big test in your near future? Do you have a job interview coming up? Are there tryouts for a sports team or a big dance coming up at school? It's easy to get caught up in worrying, stressing and planning—so much so, that you can lose out on the joy of the day and of the big events themselves. The best way to enjoy these experiences and to get the most from them is to savor the moment, to "live in the here and now." The moment is the truest—and safest—place to live.

Taste-berry promise for the day: I will live in the moment and make the most of it.

Have Integrity

*I*ntegrity is being right with yourself—no secrets, no hidden agenda, no dishonesty, just "what you see is what you get." Wearing your heart on your sleeve is not such a bad practice.

Jennifer Leigh Youngs
Taste Berries for Teens

You feel good about yourself when you are honest about who you are and what you believe in. When you act according to these personal truths, you are right with yourself and no one can take this away from you. Even if someone disagrees with you, if you're okay with your position, then you're at peace with exactly the right person. While the opinion of others isn't what matters most, you'll find that when you act with this level of integrity, you are sure to attract the admiration of many. Best of all, you secure a reputation with yourself as worthy of admiration. Be someone you can admire.

Taste-berry promise for the day: I will act according to what I believe in.

Resolve to Move On

A loss is just a loss, so don't fret over it forever. Deal with it, and then get on with your next endeavor. Your finest achievement always lies ahead.

Mark Whitman, 17
Taste Berries for Teens

Losses, failures and mistakes never produce good feelings, but don't get mired in self-pity or paralyzed by feelings of inadequacy. Instead, give yourself time to grieve and heal, then resolve to move on. Moving on means evaluating what happened, seeing what lessons you can take from the experience and regrouping. Then it's time to get on with your next goal. Every day is a chance to begin again, to start fresh. Vow to do better and be better. It's the taste-berry way.

Taste-berry promise for the day: I will make two columns on a sheet of paper, and in the first column write down what I've learned from some of my mistakes and in the second column write how I'm using it to go forward, to do and be better.

Watch for Turning Points

§pectacular or beautiful, heartrending or bewildering, some moments literally change the way you look at life.

Bettie B. Youngs
Taste Berries for Teens #3

Some moments we never forget: spectacular ones that excite us, beautiful ones that move us, harrowing ones that grip us. Although they are different experiences, each share the power to change us. Some turning points are blatant, such as a victory that brings new confidence or an unexpected defeat that makes us face self and truth, while other turning points are subtle—the realization that one's life is unhappy and empty, or lacking zest, zeal or meaning. Yet each is crucial because the insight gained has the power to put the rest of our lives in focus. These experiences can change the way we think about ourselves, even the purpose of our lives. Take time to reflect on those times that changed your view of things. The power of such moments is that they give us a glimpse of our potential as human beings.

Taste-berry promise for the day: I will journal on the insights that have changed my life.

Protect Your Heart

The human heart is quite vulnerable, very fragile, and often extremely sensitive. You really have to look out for it.

Amber Leigh, 17
Taste Berries for Teens

You are always responsible for taking care of your heart. So watch out for it: Share it with people you love. Don't ever give it away *completely.* This doesn't mean not to be open with others or share what's going on with those you trust. Rather, it means stand guard over your heart in risky situations, and nurse it back to health when it's sad or broken. Do those things that make it happy and strive to keep it healthy. Caring for your tender heart is a most noble goal and so very worth it. *You're* worth it. What are those things that make your heart skip with joy?

Taste-berry promise for the day: I will identify five ways I "look out" for my heart.

Learn Something New

Learning is the heart of growing up—and forever staying young-at-heart.

Jennifer Leigh Youngs
Taste Berries for Teens

Do you like to learn? Have you ever been so interested in learning about something that it held you spellbound? Watch closely for such times. The signals you get when enjoying something so much that you lose all track of time could be pointing your heart in the direction of fulfillment. You may be looking into the face of your *calling*. The real nature of learning is not so much filling up your head as lighting a fire within you. What you do, and most especially how you do it, often reveals not only who you are but what you need. Strive to be a lifelong learner. Be book smart, yes, but focus on uncovering your calling.

Taste-berry promise for the day: I will be a "spellbound" student today!

Define Your Success

eing a "success in life" means different things to different people. What's important is that you've decided what it means for you.

Chris Burke
A Taste-Berry Teen's Guide to Setting & Achieving Goals

What's your definition of success? Do you think "success" means amassing great wealth? Does it mean having fame or popularity? Or maybe, to you, success means having just a few friends with truly deep bonds. Does it mean creating a close-knit family? Is it accomplishing spectacular feats? Perhaps it's being at the top of your field in a chosen career. Maybe your definition of success is some inner prize, such as acquiring serenity and living in integrity. Chances are it's some combination of the above. You can see that there are many different definitions of success. How you define success can be far different from how someone else defines it. Respecting another person's definition is all well and good, but finding your own is far more important. Reflect on what is *very,* very important to you.

Taste-berry promise for the day: I will think about three ways in which I wish to be successful.

Forgive Yourself

orgive yourself for goof-ups. No one can be cool all of the time.

Jennifer Leigh Youngs
Taste Berries for Teens #3

Are you perfect yet? Are you cool all the time? Join the crowd. Accept the fact that you're human, and therefore you aren't perfect—and that's perfectly okay. When you forgive yourself for your foibles, you're better able to forgive others, and you're also better able to allow others to forgive you. Forgiveness often means letting go of some things, such as unrealistic expectations. It can even mean letting go of an old identity—you know, the one where you weren't cool unless you were perfect.

Taste-berry promise for the day: I will remember that goof-ups are part of growing up.

Share Kind Words

on't underestimate the power of kind words: They are among those things that can help make the world a "better place."

Jessica Mossage, 17
Taste Berries for Teens #3

Have you ever felt really down, but then someone said something kind and it cheered you up? Words, like acts of kindness, can uplift you and change your sense of things. Do your part: Fill the air with your hopeful, optimistic and positive thoughts, words and deeds. Even if you feel like you're a lone voice, remember that you are not. However we understand the wonder of the human family, we are interconnected: When even one of our members is lifted into a "better place," we all benefit. Be a taste berry: Do your part—share the power of uplifting words.

Taste-berry promise for the day: I will share only kind words.

The Power of Love

If only we could love deeply enough and sustain love long enough, we could become the source of our own miracles.

Jennifer Leigh Youngs
More Taste Berries for Teens

Have you ever been in love? Didn't it make you feel as if you wanted to do your very best—and that you actually could? Didn't it seem to make the world brighter, give you enthusiasm and make you feel purposeful? We are told that love is the most potent force in the entire world. Perhaps it is. For sure it is the source of many great miracles. It can transform apathy into enthusiasm, fear into faith, conflict into peace, judgment into compassion. Nurture the love that resides within your heart, knowing it has the power to create wonderful transformations in your life, in the lives of others and in the world. The essence of a taste berry is the beginning of a miracle in the making.

Taste-berry promise for the day: I will believe in miracles.

Express Your Gratitude

Gratitude becomes a circle of love.

Tina Moreno
A Teen's Guide to Living Drug-Free

When we help others, we become more grateful. And when we feel grateful, we're looking at all the good in our lives and feeling as if we have plenty—and so we want to give to others. Then, when we do just that, we inspire gratitude in them—and so we create a circle of loving gratitude. When you choose to see the world through grateful eyes and you feel as if you have so much in your life, you cannot help but want to share it with others. Do your best to keep the circle expanding: Give and grow in gratitude and love. Ask yourself, "Do I express gratitude? In what ways could I experience more gratitude in my life?"

Taste-berry promise for the day: I will tell five people why I feel grateful that they are in my life.

Leave Your Comfort Zone

When you feel overwhelmed, just remember that for eagles, too, it's the price of flying!

Bettie B. Youngs
Taste Berries for Teens

The mother eagle makes her nest high on a cliff's edge. So high, in fact, that the baby eagle is literally so terrified of its "free fall" that it will not leave the nest unless pushed out by its mother! Imagine the confusion of the baby eagle when his mother, who up to this point has been nurturing and attentive, suddenly seems to turn on him, pushing him from the nest and forcing him to fly! But, of course, in the end, pushed from the confines of a nest now outgrown, the baby eagle takes flight—and learns that everything's going to be okay. Because, you see, in the free fall, the young eagle learns to trust its wings! It's an important lesson: When your challenges seem overwhelming, when you feel frightened or confused, when you're being called to leave behind something familiar but outgrown, remember the baby eagle. You, too, can soar—but first you'll have to leave the safety of your comfort zone! Momentary "overwhelm" is to be expected, so don't let it stop you from reaching new heights in your life.

Taste-berry promise for the day: I will not fear the price of learning to "fly"! I will take one positive action that is outside my comfort zone.

Accept Others as They Are

When I start to get critical of someone, I remind myself that this person is perfectly loved by God, just as he or she is. This has a really positive effect on me. When I start to get critical of myself, I now remind myself that I, too, am perfectly loved by God—as is.

Wynnona Reyes, 15
More Taste Berries for Teens

Looking for the good and choosing not to dwell on the negative help us become more caring and loving individuals—toward others and toward ourselves. When we accept others just as they are—no matter how different from us—then we are better able to accept ourselves in spite of our inadequacies. The less we judge others, choosing to practice tolerance instead, the less critical and judgmental we are of ourselves. And the more we concentrate on looking for the good in others, the more we will see the good in ourselves, as well. Whenever you have trouble with this loving outlook, just ask the source of all love and good to remind you.

Taste-berry promise for the day: I will list ten things that are great about me.

Live Drug-Free

eing drug-free gives you a better chance to discover your true identity.

Bettie B. Youngs
A Teen's Guide to Living Drug-Free

What matters most to you? How do you feel about your life and all that is going on? Who are your "true" friends, and why? What do you want to do with your life—and how will you go about achieving all that you want? As you would expect, sorting out the "real" answers to each of these questions takes time and introspection. It also means you'll need to be at your best. Clear, heartfelt thinking is required. You'll have a better chance of knowing yourself and finding the answers to these questions when you're completely "present"—when you're not clouded under by the influence of chemicals. Being drug-free, you get to live fully. Don't miss out on finding "real" answers to "real" life. Don't miss out on being the "real" you.

Taste-berry promise for the day: I will think of the words for my own standard comeback for saying "No!" to drugs.

Be in Charge of Your Life

*Setting and achieving goals is about self-discipline.
Dare to be in charge of your life.*

Jennifer Leigh Youngs
A Taste-Berry Teen's Guide to Setting & Achieving Goals

When you are diligent about working toward your goals, you reap the satisfaction of seeing them completed. It's a cycle of success: Achievement is a good feeling; you've applied yourself and have been successful—you are deserving. "Earning" success is sure to boost your self-confidence, which will inspire you to set new goals and work toward them. Is it any wonder that your self-esteem—which is the reputation you hold of yourself— soars? This is the payoff of taking responsibility to be in charge of your life. So go for it! Dare to be someone who is disciplined about going after a life filled with worthy goals, filled with the anticipation of accomplishing interesting and purposeful activity. Make yours a life filled with promise.

Taste-berry promise for the day: I will review my goals and see that I'm "on track" toward achieving them.

Kindness Is a Taste-Berry Action

indness is one of the most profound gifts you can give. Personally, I've never met anyone who didn't want to receive it.

Carrie Hague, 15
Taste Berries for Teens

Kindness is not hard to understand, nor does it have to be difficult to practice. It can be as simple as scooting over and inviting someone to share your seat on the bus; stopping to help someone pick up a stack of dropped pencils, papers and books; introducing yourself to the new person in your school and offering directions to classes; offering to help your little brother or sister with homework; or doing *more* than your share of house and yard work for your mom or dad. Each of these acts is easy enough for you to do, yet all of them, as well as countless other "simple things," can truly mean something to someone else. Carry out these acts of kindness—these taste-berry actions—and do them with joy.

Taste-berry promise for the day: I will do something special for someone and do it joyfully.

Share Your Faith

I **can't think of any gift that is greater to share than your faith.**

Sadie Murray, 15
Taste Berries for Teens

We share so much with others—a kind word, an act of kindness, our support and advice. What can be more profound than sharing our faith, our sense of how we are connected to a Higher Power? We can witness our faith in words, of course, but we can also share it by the way we live our words. After all, our actions speak as eloquently and clearly as do our words. Demonstrate your faith for others with the way you live your life.

Taste-berry promise for the day: I will demonstrate my faith in the way I treat others.

Little Things Matter

𝒫robably we don't always know when the little things we do make a difference to others, but that doesn't make them any less important.

Jennifer Leigh Youngs
Taste Berries for Teens Journal

Has someone ever put an arm around you when you were afraid? Has someone smiled at you when you were feeling out of place? Has someone offered you a shoulder when your heart was broken? When a person is feeling sad or hurt, the loneliness of the moment can be eased by the kind word of a friend or the sincere smile of a stranger. If we each took the time to simply connect in the most effortless and uncomplicated ways, we could have an impact for the good on those fellow travelers we chance to encounter on this journey of life. Continue to do those little things that can make immeasurable differences in the souls of those you help.

Taste-berry promise for the day: I will make eye contact and wish others a good day.

Help Someone

I know what it's like to have lost your way, and how important it is to find someone who will show you a new way.

Lisa Cartwright, 16
Taste Berries for Teens

Have you ever felt as if you've "lost your way"? Have you ever had someone reach out and help you get back on course? If so, you know how much it meant—what a difference it made to you. Great joy and satisfaction can be found in reaching out and making a positive difference in the life of someone who has "lost her way." It can help to keep in mind that, from time to time, we all lose our way. Do you remember your feelings of gratitude, hope and strength when someone was there to show you your "new way"? Be a source of such gratitude, hope and strength for others. A taste-berry approach is to remember that everyone is a student of life as well as a teacher.

Taste-berry promise for the day: I will reach out to help someone, reminding myself that I am both a student and a teacher.

Inspire Yourself

By being positive and not putting myself down, I actually help myself do better. I like it when other people encourage me, so it only makes sense that I encourage me, too.

Dan Belana, 17
Taste Berries for Teens

Be a source of your own inspiration! Look for all the ways you can encourage yourself: Applaud yourself when you've completed a difficult task or a long assignment; congratulate yourself when you've done an especially good or thorough job; commend yourself when you've been kind or acted with integrity. Don't dwell on your losses and don't be your own worst critic—instead try being your own cheerleader. When you're a taste berry to yourself—doing and taking note of the positive—not only will you feel good about yourself, but you're far more apt to be a source of inspiration to others.

Taste-berry promise for the day: I will create my own personal "cheer" and say it to myself.

61

Be Sensitive to Moods

Sometimes we just need others to be sensitive and understanding—even gentle with us—as we work through our moods.

Bettie B. Youngs
Taste Berries for Teens

We all have our ups and downs. It's just a normal part of being human. Just as we have our "up-and-on" days, so we can have those "down-and-out" days. Make it your goal to have the "up-and-on" days outweigh the "down-and-out" ones, and work with yourself to better "manage" your disposition on those "off days." And don't forget that you can help others to be gentle and sensitive to your moods—to "cut you a little slack"—if you give them a "heads-up" on how you're feeling. When you say something like, "Thanks for being patient with me today. For some reason, I'm having a tough time getting it together," you communicate how you'd like them to treat you. And, remember, when someone else is having their own "off day," be sensitive and respectful of their feelings, as well.

Taste-berry promise for the day: I will be patient with me and respectful of the moods of others.

Be a Can-Do Person

Achievement is a brilliant contribution to self-worth!

Mark Whitman, 17
Taste Berries for Teens

Setting goals and applying determination and hard work are the routes to getting things accomplished. When you've set a goal and achieved it, the message that you send to yourself is that you are a "can-do" person. Self-efficacy—the "I-am-a-capable-and-competent-person" statement—is a powerful building block for creating positive self-esteem. Self-esteem—the image you hold of yourself—is an important reflection, because just about everything you say and do stems from this picture. The good news is that you have a say in this self-portrait— because the paintbrush is in your hands. Don't forget to add the "color" of achievement when you're painting a picture of yourself! Ask yourself, "In what ways am I a 'can-do' person?"

Taste-berry promise for the day: I will journal on all the ways I am a capable person.

Day 64

Be a Loving Person

Being loved affirms that we are loveable—we are wanted. Giving love gives us a purpose—we are needed. But we must first love ourselves in order to experience either of these feelings.

Bettie B. Youngs
More Taste Berries for Teens

Some say that of all the things we do in our lifetimes, the most important is learning to be a loving person—to see life and circumstances through the eyes of our hearts. With each new test, trial and triumph, we learn new lessons on the importance of love—both on the value of receiving it and of sharing it. Yet "Love 101"—the prerequisite for all love's lessons—stresses the importance of loving ourselves. We are each love's student. Ask yourself, "In what ways do I experience and express love?" In sorting through the answers, keep in mind that all of love's lessons are valuable.

Taste-berry promise for the day: I will list three things I believe about the importance and power of love, and think over a lesson I'm currently "learning."

Day 65

Honor Your Body

It's a proven fact: You are what you eat.

Jennifer Leigh Youngs
Feeling Great, Looking Hot & Loving Yourself! Health, Beauty and Fitness for Teens

Health experts say, "We are what we eat." True enough! If you have a soda and a donut for breakfast, chances are you'll have a hyper morning and by second period experience the effects of the sugar wearing off. A healthy diet is important to good health. Your body needs nutritious foods in order to regulate body functions, promote growth, repair body tissues and, of course, get energy. Honor your body: Fuel it so it can do its job. Respect yourself enough to make healthy choices about the food you eat. Your body depends on you to preserve its life and nourish its source of energy. Remember, you are your body's most important taste berry. And taking care of yourself assures that you will be there to take care of others.

Taste-berry promise for the day: I will plan three healthy meals to nourish my body.

Seek Personal Growth

he person you see today is not necessarily the you of next year. We recreate ourselves all the time.

Bettie B. Youngs
Taste Berries for Teens

We are always in a state of "being" and "becoming." Know that as you grow and change, you can choose to direct that "being" and "becoming." Recreating yourself is about continually making choices about what sort of a person you'd like to become. Think about some of the people you admire and respect. In what ways are they smart, funny and friendly—and how can you enhance those qualities in yourself? You always have a choice to *improve* yourself. Just as you think about the way you wear your hair and the color and style of the clothes you purchase, you can make choices about your attitude, thinking and behavior as well. So go ahead: Start on your "new and improved" self today. Personal growth is a personal choice.

Taste-berry promise for the day: I will tell my best friend the qualities I'd like to have and the details of who I'd like to "become."

Share a Smile!

A smile can be the start of falling in love.

Erin Bishop, 17
Taste Berries for Teens

A smile is a universal language—one with awesome power. It's not surprising what a smile can do! A mere smile can stop someone's tears and lift the mood of a person feeling sorrowful, comfort discouragement and dissolve loneliness. A smile can even be the catalyst for falling in love! Here's more good news: You don't have to be the same age or speak the same language to share the far-reaching influence of a smile. So share one today, starting by smiling at the face looking back in your mirror. If you're feeling particularly communicative today, share one with everyone you meet! You'll find the results taste-berry sweet: You're more approachable with a friendly face (versus a gloomy one)—and smiling will encourage others to get to know you better.

Taste-berry promise for the day: I will smile at everyone I meet—beginning with the face in the mirror.

Take Charge of Your Life

Don't be a passive bystander in your life! Get in the game—the sooner the better.

J. J. Bailey, 17
A Taste-Berry Teen's Guide to Setting & Achieving Goals

Sometimes it can be easy to think that we have little to no control over what happens, but nothing could be farther from the truth. While others certainly have a say in things, you're in charge of the direction of your life. It begins by thinking about the sort of life you'd like to live and making some decisions about your willingness to do what it takes to bring that about. So the sky being the limit, dream your dreams, capture them in the way of goals. What do you want: good friends, good grades, playing sports, a good relationship with your mom and dad, a spectacular future? You can have these things. They begin with the choices you make. So don't be passive: Even if your life seems hampered by obstacles and challenges, all these are but mere stepping stones to becoming stronger and more determined to create the life you want. Believe that you can do it. Start shaping the direction of your life today.

Taste-berry promise for the day: I will journal about the sort of life I'd like to live.

Day 69

Approve of Yourself

*B*eing drug-free is the best chance you have to be in an authentic relationship with others—and most especially, with yourself.

Tina Moreno
A Teen's Guide to Living Drug-Free

The more authentic you are in coping with the things going on in your life, the more you approve of yourself. Self-esteem is the basis for approving of yourself, and for the satisfaction you feel with practically everything else going on in life. Being drug-free, your sense of self-worth is whole and intact, so you're better able to take things in stride and see things clearly. This helps you to balance the good with the bad, the ups with the downs: You make allowances for one day feeling on top of the world, and the next day, barely hanging in there. You're okay with both, knowing it's just the way life is and that you need not deny, nor self-medicate, the experience.

Taste-berry promise for the day: I will consider the ways I approve of myself and remain committed to living drug-free.

Treasure Your Family

Care about your brothers and sisters—everywhere.

Nick Maldonado, 16
More Taste Berries for Teens

We often set our best table for company. Doing special things for others is certainly nice. But just as we do nice things for our "brothers and sisters" in the world, we must not forget to also do nice things for the brothers and sisters with whom we live every day. How are you a taste berry to your brothers and sisters at home—how do you "set your best table" for them? Do you do this by speaking kindly, being helpful, assisting with homework and explaining the love behind the family "rules"? When you do such things, you model love and consideration. So do all you can to show love to the members of your family: Not only will this cement a relationship of love between you forever, but it will help them prepare to be taste berries within the family they may create, as well as to their brothers and sisters in the community and in the world as well.

Taste-berry promise for the day: I will volunteer to help out at home with extra chores.

Seek Support from Others

Lean on others when you need help and support.

Lindsay Moody, 15
Taste Berries for Teens #3

Have you ever felt insecure about something, but didn't want to let on about it? Have there been times when you felt depressed, sad, afraid, hurt or alone? Allowing others to comfort, support and care for you in such times is a sign of being mature and responsible. It takes strength of character to put aside false pride and get the support you need to work through emotion-laden issues. The next time you're going through a tough moment, share it with someone you trust. Not only will it ease the weight of the way you're feeling, but it will make another person feel needed, as well. People like to be wanted and needed by each other. Wanting to be a taste berry is a natural thing for most of us. Give others this opportunity: Go to them for support.

Taste-berry promise for the day: I will ask someone I trust to be part of my support system.

Surrender Control

Oh, the time and energy I might have saved if I had turned my crisis over to Spirit to begin with!

Christian Sorensen
More Taste Berries for Teens

Have you tried to make something work and it just "wasn't happening"? At times we may need to stop struggling and simply "let go." This isn't always easy. We feel like if we just do something, force something, change something, we will be in control and things will get better. But the truth is none of us are in control of *everything*. Often, the surrender of "letting go" is what is needed in order for things to change for the better. What do you need to let go of?

Taste-berry promise for the day: I will journal about those things I can't control and how I can "let go" of them.

You Can Get Through Tough Times

Eventually one learns to see that no matter how bad things get, there is always "light at the end of the tunnel."

Shawn McLaughlin, 17
Taste Berries for Teens

Sometimes when a situation looks tough, whether it be an overwhelming schedule or a broken heart, you may question your ability to get through it. Know that you can—and will. Sometimes it's the slow plodding of putting one foot in front of the other and encouraging yourself that gets you slowly but surely to the other side of a difficult situation. Once on the other side, renewed hope takes over: You made it! You survived! You can get through tough times! Once you've learned this, share your hopeful experience with others who are walking through their own dark days. "It'll get better," you can promise and encourage, knowing with absolute certainty that it truly will. Because experience has taught you there is "light at the end of the tunnel"!

Taste-berry promise for the day: I will let someone who is struggling know that eventually it will get better.

Cut Parents Some Slack!

Parents are learning as they go along, so it can't hurt to "cut them some slack."

Joanna Kameran, 16
Taste Berries for Teens #3

Of course you love your parents and appreciate all they do for you. But sometimes, let's face it, parents can ask too many questions, overmanage your time and say "no" more than "yes"! It can be frustrating. Short of finding an apartment, moving out and getting a job to support yourself, what can you do? For starters, you can cut your parents a little slack! Here's why: Just as being a teen is characterized by new and first-time experiences, being a parent is new territory as well. Each new day and each new you is a first for them—just as it is for you. When you went out on your first date, that was the first time your parents experienced their teen going out on a date, too. And the first time you took the family car for a spin—they were jittery, as well. In each new experience, your parents are feeling as new and inexperienced as you. They may sometimes make mistakes, but work with them—they have your very best interests at heart! On those days when you're feeling more grown up than they've noticed, listen with an open heart. Throughout it all, remember how unbreakable the loving ties to your parents really are—regardless of whether each is a "perfect" parent or still just trying to be.

Taste-berry promise for the day: I will thank my parents for standing by all my learning experiences.

Tough Times Deepen Compassion

Tough times can teach us to be compassionate.

Jennifer Leigh Youngs
Taste Berries for Teens #3

Have you ever been deeply saddened by the death of a beloved friend or family member? Have you ever had a close friend go through something similar? Experiencing heartache or going through a painful struggle often leads to a new depth of compassion within you. Seeing someone else who is struggling with a difficult situation, you realize how much this person is hurting, just like you—and you know how bad it feels. But you also know that your comfort, support and understanding are needed: Having weathered your own suffering, grief, guilt or other painful feelings, you are better able to understand what others are facing. What a remarkable knowing: Our own compassion is deepened because of our tough times and can therefore be used to ease the pain of others. Be a taste berry: Practice being compassionate to those who are struggling with painful feelings.

Taste-berry promise for the day: I will offer to help someone who is struggling with a difficult situation.

Look for Life's Gifts

Experience has taught me that I shouldn't take things for granted.

Erin Bishop, 17
Taste Berries for Teens

Do you sometimes get so busy that you take all the good things in your life for granted—the love of family, time with friends, a home, enough food to eat and a chance to go to school? You may be deserving of all these things, but they still shouldn't be taken for granted. And there's even more to this than just the fact that everyone's life does not include these things, so you should be grateful because you have them: Gratitude grants your life deeper joy and meaning. Sometimes just a moment filled with blessings is enough. You get up in the morning, taking in a deep breath of air, and hear the birds singing outside your window, as well as your family stirring as they begin their day. You smile knowing you share your home with other loving heartbeats. In this moment, you realize all these gifts are good—and this moment is enough. Learn to look for the gifts in your life and to be grateful for those times when even the moment is enough.

Taste-berry promise for the day: I will make a list of those things for which I am grateful.

Know Your Support System

K̸now who is in your camp and on your side. This sup-port system can make you feel as though you can take on the world.

Bettie B. Youngs
A Taste-Berry Teen's Guide to Managing the Stress and Pressures of Life

When life doles out stress, pressure and tough times, the support of friends and family is the surest way to help you feel that even if everything comes crashing down around your head, you'll be okay. Your "support system"—those who need no prompting to cheer you up, motivate and inspire you, or comfort and encourage you—believe in you no matter what. So you are not alone. You still have what matters, and those you need the most are still with you. What a comfort. When you are in the middle of a crisis, who are the taste berries you turn to for support? Know who they are.

Taste-berry promise for the day: I will make a list of five people who love and care about me, and journal on all the ways they support me.

Be Kind to Animals

The creatures on our planet depend on us, too!

Danny Joseph, 15
Taste Berries for Teens

When you come across a lost, abandoned or neglected animal, how do you feel? Do you think it's someone else's responsibility to rescue it and take it to the animal shelter, or do you feel that since you've happened upon it, it's your role to protect it from being hurt and help it reach safety? Ponder this question: Could it be that all creatures on the planet are in some way interdependent? Regardless of how you speak or understand the mystery, all of life is "connected." Be a taste berry: If you have a pet, take good care of it, and be kind to it. If you see a lost or abandoned animal, call the Humane Society or animal shelter. Be someone who looks out for our feathered or furry friends.

Taste-berry promise for the day: I will offer to walk an elderly neighbor's dog.

The Real Definition of "Cool"

People who feel really good about themselves are the safest people to be around.

Rita Sultanyan, 14
Taste Berries for Teens

Have you ever noticed how many genuinely cool people are both kind to others and also very confident about themselves? When people feel really comfortable about who they are and their own worth, they don't feel the need to put others down. Envy, jealousy and insecurity are wiped out of their relationships, and they are left without motives for hurting someone else. This doesn't mean that everyone who feels bad about themselves gets satisfaction out of putting other people down; rather, it means that most people who get satisfaction out of hurting others don't feel good about themselves. Knowing this can also encourage you to examine your own motives when you've put someone else down. You can then work on both apologizing and doing all you can so you don't repeat your mistake. When you feel really good about yourself, you're sure to be a better taste berry to others. Do those things that make you feel good about yourself—everyone benefits from it.

Taste-berry promise for the day: I will praise a success someone else has accomplished.

Be a Hero

eroes are just regular folks with one exception: When someone needs help, they help.

Casey Igo, 15
Taste Berries for Teens #3

How many heroes have you had in your life? Who was there to lend you a helping hand when you fell down and skinned your knees as a child? Wasn't that person your hero in that moment? Who took the time to teach you the schoolwork you just couldn't seem to grasp in class? Wouldn't it be fair to say that this person was acting as your hero in this situation? Who helped you clean up the huge mess when you spilled your lunch tray in the middle of the cafeteria? This person, too, became your hero! Help those who need it as you go through your day—then you, too, will be a hero. All it takes is desire. As Ralph Waldo Emerson said, "A hero is not braver than an ordinary man, but he is braver five minutes longer."

Taste-berry promise for the day: I will reserve space in my journal or scrapbook especially for recording those moments I was a hero.

Be a Positive Person

It's more fun to be with someone who looks for the good in others, than to be with someone who puts everyone down.

Shawn Hamilton, 16
Taste Berries for Teens

Think of the people you know who are the most fun to be around. Usually they are people who are good to others and who see their lives in a positive light. They love to laugh, but not at the expense of others. They naturally look for the best in you, as well as in everyone else. Being around them is uplifting; it makes you feel good about yourself and life in general. On the other hand, if you're around someone who is constantly criticizing, judging and putting others down, soon enough you'll find your own spirits suffering. Just as you find it uplifting to be around positive people, be a taste berry to others: By your example lift them to better thoughts, feelings and actions.

Taste-berry promise for the day: I will list the three best qualities about each member of my family and my two closest friends.

People Need People

Being with others makes our world sizzle: We are a part of something—accepted, needed and loved.

Bettie B. Youngs
More Taste Berries for Teens

Nothing could ring more true than the sentiment, "People need people." When you are with others your life just bubbles with more energy and meaning. Doing things with others adds new dimension to life, as it brings you a deeper awareness that you are part of the greater whole of humanity and you have a secure place in it. Bouncing ideas off others, listening to what they have to say and how they feel, even simply sharing silence, we humans innately desire to be with others. Be someone who sizzles with positive energy: Do and say those things that make being in the presence of others a positive and enlightening experience.

Taste-berry promise for the day: I will make plans to spend time openly sharing from my heart with my friends this weekend.

Find True Friends

A friend is someone with whom we can relax and just hang out, have fun and share our innermost thoughts—deep dark secrets, lofty and noble goals, or our hopes, joys and fears.

Jennifer Leigh Youngs
Taste Berries for Teens

It's such a comfort and a freedom to know you can simply be yourself with your friends, and your friends will love and support you as you are. It's great to have someone to share the full spectrum of your thoughts, feelings, dreams and ideas—someone with whom you know it is safe to share your lows, as well as who will celebrate your victories as joyfully as you do. Not only does this kind of friendship enrich your own life, but it makes the world richer for its presence. This is the sort of friendship we should always cherish, and the sort of friend we should always seek to be. Remember, the building of such friendships starts with you.

Taste-berry promise for the day: I will ask my best friend to describe her dreams for the future and her greatest victories up until now.

83

Day 84

Learn from Your Mistakes

I've made mistakes in the past, and I want to learn from them and not repeat them.

Andrew Philip Kegley, 15
Taste Berries for Teens #3

Have you ever been caught cheating, telling a "white lie" or been pulled over to the side of the road by a police officer? All are consequences of having made some bad decisions. Still, these "mistakes" can be used to become a better person. How? By vowing not to repeat a "poor decision" and by learning from the mistakes you've made. Ask yourself: What are the lessons this taught me? What amends do I need to make? How can I use what I've learned to become a better person? What is the biggest mistake you've ever made, and what is the lesson you learned? In what ways are you now a "better" person for having learned from your mistake?

Taste-berry promise for the day: I will journal on the two most important lessons I've learned from my biggest mistake.

The Courage to Do the Right Thing

Have the courage to do what is right all the time.

Nancy Robins, 14
More Taste Berries for Teens

Have you ever gone to an activity, such as an ice-skating rink or the fair, where the price of admission goes up right at your age? It would be easy to say you were a year younger and save a lot of money—that's what all of your friends are doing. What would *you* do? Oftentimes it takes true courage to do what is right, especially when it means not going along with the crowd. If you've been in a similar situation, you know it can be tough to do the right thing. Do it anyway. Your friends will come to know you as someone who has the courage to do what is right. And it may be that your modeling this courage for them assures that you won't be the only one "doing what is right" the next time!

Taste-berry promise for the day: I will look in the mirror and tell myself, "I commit to doing what I know is right."

Strengthen Your Faith

Faith is not something we put on, but it's carried inside of us.

Debbie Thurman
A Teen's Guide to Christian Living

Faith, to some, is a catchall word for any belief that works for us. But faith is not something we put on; it's carried inside of us. Faith does not exist in a vacuum. It means nothing unless it is both freely given to—and received by—a source that is unshakeable and unchangeable under any circumstances. We bring the *idea* of faith or trust down to our level when we speak of the reliability of a person or an event, for example. You are being asked to place your faith in a leader when you go to the polls at the age of eighteen and older to vote. The faith that defines our relationship with God may seem like that same kind of everyday faith. Yet, there is one important difference: God is incapable of failing, changing or breaking a promise. He is Truth. He is Fact. He is the Source. Strengthen your faith by feeding your heart and soul and connecting with God.

Taste-berry promise for the day: I will devote ten minutes of my day to reading inspirational literature.

Agree to Disagree

You don't always have to be right, as long as you do what's right.

BeShawn Niles, 13
Taste Berries for Teens

There's a big danger in always having to be right. It can cause you to nurse a grudge and waste energy trying to convince others of your case, whatever it may be. It almost always includes proving that someone else is wrong, which rarely creates an atmosphere of respect. There's no shame in admitting you've made a mistake, and there's a great deal of honor in offering to "agree to disagree." Moving past the need to be right, you can get back to the business of doing what is right—which means acting with integrity and living in peace with others.

Taste-berry promise for the day: I will offer to "agree to disagree" in a case where I'm in conflict with someone else.

Be Honest with Yourself

*Being honest with yourself is a quality—and value—
that builds your relationships with others.*

Wyatt Atkins, 16
A Teen's Guide to Living Drug-Free

Have you ever convinced yourself that something was all right when deep inside you knew that it really wasn't? It can be something that seems harmless; for example, is it possible that the lead singer at the rock concert wasn't really singing right to you? It's so important to be honest with ourselves—even seemingly "small" lies begin to erode our sense of trust in ourselves. And if you're not honest with yourself, you can't be honest with other people. Not only does being honest with yourself improve your relationships with others, but it allows you to learn and grow from your mistakes and builds your self-esteem. It's great to "own" this kind of honesty. Make it yours today.

Taste-berry promise for the day: I will be honest with others by being honest with myself.

Be a Good Friend

A good friend helps you become a better, wiser and more compassionate person than you might have been without that person in your life.

Jennifer Leigh Youngs
Taste Berries for Teens

How do babies learn to talk? How do toddlers learn to share? How do we learn manners as we grow older? We learn all these by watching others. We learn them by example. It is in this same way that our friends teach us kindness and compassion. When someone is there for you, listens to your ups and downs, your hopes and dreams, your concerns and problems, when they offer support and guidance and tell you the honest truth about "what's up," they are an example of all they offer, an example of a true taste berry. Such modeling teaches you to provide the same example in return. Good friendships are a winning proposition: Not only do you have someone to teach you how to be the best you possible, you also have someone with whom you can put into practice all those lessons that you've learned on being a taste berry.

Taste-berry promise for the day: I will act as a good example of compassion to my friends.

It Feels Good to Help Others

Help others. The effects will be far-reaching.

Jennifer Leigh Youngs
Taste Berries for Teens Journal

A group of seniors in Holland, Michigan, opted to help others, rather than play a standard senior prank. Arriving at school on lawn tractors, packing their own hoses and weed trimmers, some students circled the school ceremonially then set to work mowing, planting flowers and washing windows. Others in the group handed out snacks and drinks—and spirited fun—as a way to boost the morale of their fellow students. Unexpected ideas for ways to give and help others serve as great taste-berry twists from which we can all gain inspiration for being more creative in our own efforts. Helping others—whether in your family, your school or your community—has great payoffs for everyone.

Taste-berry promise for the day: I will brainstorm with a friend about fun and creative ways to help others.

Be a Shepherd

Be a lamp, or a lifeboat, or a ladder. Help someone's soul heal. Walk out of your house like a shepherd.

Rumi
Taste Berries for Teens #3

Such touching images: "a lamp," there to shine and light the way; "a lifeboat," there to rescue; "a ladder," there to provide a way up and out. Perhaps most beautiful is the philosopher and poet Rumi's impassioned request, "Walk out of your house like a shepherd"—a shepherd being someone who is dedicated to guiding, protecting and looking after his flock. How healing it could be to the entire world if each day, when we leave our homes, we would practice his words—our hearts willing to be pleasant and helpful. And, how healing it could be for the "shepherd" as well. When you leave your home today, seek to be a shepherd to those who you meet throughout your day.

Taste-berry promise for the day: I will offer to lead a school project designed to help others.

We Are the World

Moving from "me" to "you" is an entirely new per-spective, and when practiced, an entirely new level of living.

Bettie B. Youngs
More Taste Berries for Teens

When we get beyond focusing solely on our own needs and desires, it's as if a whole new universe opens up. "Me" reaching out to "you" becomes "us" or "we"—a unity that is greater than any solitary self-centered existence. Think about it: Isn't the outcome of an assignment different if it's a group project rather than when you're required to do it on your own? Connection invites greater perspective, deeper meaning and a fuller level of contentment. Practice "we" each and every day: at home, at school and in your community. Like the song affirms, *"We are the world."* If we all embrace this truth, an entirely new level of living will open for everyone on the planet.

Taste-berry promise for the day: I will call the local community center to ask how I can be of help in my community.

Words of Encouragement

*aying a kind or encouraging word can make some-
one's victory more sweet or ease the ache of a
broken heart.*

Bettie B. Youngs
Taste Berries for Teens

Do you remember a time when you pulled off a victory and someone said, "Way to go!"? How about a time when someone offered, "I'm sorry you're hurting," or, "Can I do anything to help?" Words of encouragement demonstrate the power of love in action. Take a moment to think of those taste berries who were there to support you and how much their words of encouragement, whether praise or comfort, meant to you. Aren't these memories poignant and empowering? Didn't you find them inspiring? Be a taste berry: Share kind and encouraging words with everyone.

Taste-berry promise for the day: I will ask someone in need how I can be of help.

Expand Your Circle of Friends

Friends: Each one is so different—which is why you need lots of them.

Barbara Allen, 14
Taste Berries for Teens

No two people are exactly the same, nor are any two friendships exactly alike. The more friends you have, and the more diverse they are, the more opportunities you have for learning and growing. So think big and expand your world by expanding your "circle" of friends. You can do so knowing that each friend can teach you new and different things about yourself. "Circle" the world of their experience and travel "full circle" right back to a new aspect of you! It's an amazing way to see fresh sights (and insights) as you travel through life!

Taste-berry promise for the day: I will share with a close friend three cool ways we are so different and how each adds to our friendship.

Radiate Inner Beauty

Feeling complete, being at peace within, is the most perfect expression of beauty.

Jennifer Leigh Youngs
Feeling Great, Looking Hot & Loving Yourself! Health, Fitness and Beauty for Teens

Do you know someone who just seems to be at peace within herself? Have you noticed the gentle yet powerful beauty this person radiates? The person may be young or old, male or female, tall or short, any build or color—such things do not matter, for inner peace shines in only one age, size, kind and color—which is "perfect as is." Feeling "complete," being at peace within, stems from believing that a power greater than yourself is at work in your life, promising that all you will ever need to face life's challenges has already been provided. Trust that this power is in charge of everything and that things will turn out as they are supposed to. Take the time to contemplate your faith; explore its presence all around you—and within you. Appreciate the beauty it bestows.

Taste-berry promise for the day: I will take five minutes of solitude and silence in order to touch the peace that lies within.

Set Specific Goals

There will always be a million and one things to do, but much of it's a waste of time. I've discovered that if you don't have specific goals, then you won't have anything to show for yourself.

Tyanna Leigh Dayton, 17
A Taste-Berry Teen's Guide to Setting & Achieving Goals

Aside from making it through the school year, can you recall your biggest accomplishments in seventh grade? Unless you had specific goals and accomplished them, chances are that year remains but a blur of activities. Every year may produce the same results. Certainly, there are a million and one activities (and distractions) that fill up your time. In order to avoid getting caught in the activity trap—where you're busy but not all that productive—set goals for the school term (or calendar year) and then create a plan to accomplish your goals. Rather than spending your time "everywhere," decide what is of most value and most worth doing. By channeling your energy into *specific* activities, not only are you more likely to achieve your goals, but when the year is over, you'll look back and see all that you've accomplished. You'll feel great about yourself, and the taste berry of self-esteem will be rooted in years and years of knowing you are a "can-do" person.

Taste-berry promise for the day: I will write my five biggest goals for the school term and three ways I will accomplish each of them.

Practice Peace

*ike every drop of water that is needed to make a con-
tainer full, each of us must do our part in seeing that
we create a peaceful world.*

Michelle Langowski, 17
Taste Berries for Teens #3

Imagine if every person on the planet was committed to peace. Imagine a world where there were no wars or any violence. Imagine if each and every one of us practiced peace in our homes, in our schools, at our work, in our communities, in our hearts—all the time. Imagine if each and every person was committed to being a taste berry to the whole of humanity—each one praying for peace, each studying and practicing ways to be culturally sensitive to others. It's a choice we each can make. When you live in peace, you help create this vision of peace in the world. Can you calculate the number of lives you've touched—possibly even changed—by being a peaceful person? Believe that your peaceful actions have power. Dare to dream of creating the peaceful world of your imagination.

Taste-berry promise for the day: I will be an "ambassador of peace" by learning all I can about other cultures in order to help promote peace.

Love Colors Everything

Love changes the color of everything.

Jennifer Leigh Youngs
Taste Berries for Teens

It's another ordinary day—classes to attend, friends to see, chores to do. There is, however, one exception: It's your birthday, and your best friend has just informed you that there will be a little party for you at her house after school. Not only will your closest friends be there, but that special someone will be there, too. Suddenly the day is not so ordinary: Love "colors" *everything and everyone* it touches. Parents, teachers, best friends and others who just admire you and think you're the best—all brighten your world with various shades of love. Don't forget to notice love in your life—and thank those who paint your days with it. Share your love with others; make "love" the color of our world.

Taste-berry promise for the day: I will think about how the love in my life "colors" my world.

Relationships and Expectations

I've never been in, or known of, a relationship that didn't have expectations of some sort.

Jennifer Leigh Youngs
Taste Berries for Teens #3

What if your best friend expected nothing of you—nor did your mom or dad, or teachers, not even your special someone? Can you imagine that feeling? What if you didn't expect anything of anyone? There would be no relationship—or at least not one you'd want to stay in. An expectation is a belief in your ability to behave in a certain way. Everyone—young and old— has expectations placed on them. It's just the way it is. Sometimes expectations can be unreasonable or unhealthy—of course, you want to watch out for this. Yet another goal can be not to always see expectations as burdensome or constraining. Such accountability can cause us to do better and be better than we might have been without someone's belief leading us to a higher, nobler place. Who are the people you love and admire the most, and what expectations do you have of them, and they of you? Allow these expectations to shape your life in positive directions, and bind your heart in love to those who give you this chance to grow.

Taste-berry promise for the day: I will list five important expectations I have for myself.

Live Your Values

Be true to what you know is right—even if you know no one else is looking.

Tomoko Ogata, 15
Taste Berries for Teens #3

Have you ever wanted to stop and help someone who looked lost or like they needed assistance, but you knew that your friends were going to be waiting somewhere for you and you didn't want to lose out on time with them? Have you ever had a cashier give you back too much change? You could easily tell yourself the store would never even miss it—but you know it wouldn't be right even if no one else ever knew that it was missing. We're confronted with value-laden "real-life" decisions every day. In order to do the right thing, you have to be honest with yourself. What are your deeply held values? Own them. Live them. Even if no one else knows whether or not you are staying true to these values, you do. When it comes to being a "taste berry," living your values is absolutely required.

Taste-berry promise for the day: I will make a list of all my deeply held values.

Life Is Sacred

*L*ove asks us to protect all life as sacred.

Bettie B. Youngs
Taste Berries for Teens

Have you ever noticed that when you come from an attitude of love, even the plight of an injured bird seems to become your own? Love is big enough to encompass and embrace all life. When you open to this kind of love, you can see that all creation is sacred and deserves to be honored and valued. As you come from this attitude of love and unity, you treat all creatures and all life with respect. Look at all the wondrous forms of life that surround you: humans, plants, trees, animals, insects—all make up creation and all are worthy of being protected by love. Be a taste berry: Protect all life as sacred.

Taste-berry promise for the day: I will "adopt" a tree, bush or flower, care for it and watch it grow.

Listen with Your Heart

If you want to have a reputation as someone who is "really levelheaded," then be someone who others feel listens with an open and unbiased mind.

Jennifer Leigh Youngs
A Taste-Berry Teen's Guide to Managing the Stress and Pressures of Life

It is a truly special feeling to know that others admire you and see you as someone who is fair and unbiased, that they can express what they're feeling without the risk of rejection. The key to maturing into a person with these qualities may well be listening with your heart, as well as with your ears. The heart knows love does not judge harshly and waits patiently for truth to be revealed—allowing the other person the dignity, the time and freedom to discover and to share just what this truth may be. Do you want to have a reputation as someone who is levelheaded? Then offer a taste berry of great worth—put all biases aside as you listen to others.

Taste-berry promise for the day: I will share with a friend what's going on for me and make it safe for him or her to do the same.

Seek Acceptance in Positive Ways

cceptance and belonging are powerful feelings within our hearts—for better or for worse, they can shape our lives.

Bettie B. Youngs
More Taste Berries for Teens

The need to belong and be accepted is part of our nature as human beings. Even so, belonging and acceptance shouldn't come at the sacrifice of your true self. Just as we can be influenced in positive ways, so too can we be influenced in negative ways. You probably find that hanging out with friends who want to be good students creates a desire in you to also be a good student, or that those friends who treat their parents with respect inspire you to do the same. Look for friends who are a positive influence. Seek acceptance and belonging with those who encourage and inspire you to be your best and do your best.

Taste-berry promise for the day: I will invite my friends to join me in doing something positive for our school.

Plan Ahead

You "direct" the outcome of your life by the things you do—and don't do—each and every day. So have a plan.

Cammie Brinthall, 15
A Taste-Berry Teen's Guide to Setting & Achieving Goals

If you don't anticipate ahead of time what you are going to wear to school tomorrow, you might get up and find that a favorite outfit isn't clean and therefore you'll have to choose something else . . . even though you'd really had your heart set on wearing that particular thing. If you don't call ahead to get all the information you need to schedule your test for your driver's license, you might get to the Department of Motor Vehicles and find a line so long you have to come another day, or you might fail to bring some document required to get your license. The same is true in most areas of your life—from planning for college to getting a job, from passing a final to going to a great concert. By planning ahead, you're in greater charge of the outcome. You're in the director's seat. Don't "run" your life in a haphazard manner. Take charge!

Taste-berry promise for the day: I'll make a plan for my day—and stick to it.

Unconditional Friends

good friend allows you a safe space to share your deepest thoughts and needs—without worry of being judged, criticized or made to feel silly for feeling the way you do.

Roma Kipling, 17
Taste Berries for Teens

Do you have a friend who you can go to with absolutely anything you are thinking and feeling, knowing this person will take what you're saying seriously and not think any less of you? When you're going through a rough spot or even just sorting through day-to-day thoughts and feelings, having someone you can trust to help sort through things is a real advantage. Knowing you'll be accepted unconditionally as you unravel the knots of your problems and deepest thoughts is a great comfort and support. Appreciate friends who create this space for you. And don't forget to be a taste berry: Return the same acceptance and friendship in full measure.

Taste-berry promise for the day: I will tell my friends, "Remember that I'm here to help if you ever need me."

Take Time to Be Alone

Take time to be alone with yourself. If you don't, how can you know yourself—much less be your own best friend?

Bettie B. Youngs
More Taste Berries for Teens

We make time to spend with our friends; time shared is often the glue that cements a relationship. Think of it: You are probably closest to those with whom you spend the most time. Just as you make time for others, it's important to take time for being alone with yourself. Time alone can help you get in touch with the real you, and to reflect on your life and assess how things are going. Time alone provides a "space" to ponder the reasons for your being and to set goals for a future you'd like to bring about. Time—such an essential element. Be sure to save some for yourself.

Taste-berry promise for the day: I will make time to be alone with myself.

Enjoy Nature's Beauty

*acred moments are astonishing because they reunite
us with profound truths.*

Jennifer Leigh Youngs
Feeling Great, Looking Hot & Loving Yourself! Health, Fitness and Beauty for Teens

Take time to notice the phenomenal array of activity going on around you—the multitude of inhabitants of nature. Notice how Mother Nature flaunts her beauty: intricately colored flowers, the sweet fragrance of blossoms, the medley of birds. Take the time to be enchanted by the floating clouds, to be mesmerized by a setting sun, and to discover even the teeniest and tiniest of wildflowers. As you witness each, be still and feel the powerful stirrings going on inside of you. Ponder that you are not alone. Day-to-day life is busy, there's so much to do, so many obligations to fulfill. Yet it's important to set aside time for "stargazing" at Mother Nature's beauty: The mystery of her splendor allows your spirit-self to notice truths bigger than your daily life. Honor such wisdom. Look to the teaching that is being revealed.

Taste-berry promise for the day: I will nourish my spirit by taking time to appreciate the beauty of nature.

Love Is a Banner

From the inside to the outside, love makes its presence known.

Bettie B. Youngs
Taste Berries for Teens

We attribute the feeling of love to our hearts. But love refuses to be contained within the heart alone. Love, like a banner written across the sky, is a bold and visible expression—and one that can be seen by all! Is there love in your life? If so, count on your heart to want to shout from the top of the mountain about its happiness and positively giddy elation over having found another little heart with whom it can commune. Have you a hurt or broken heart? If so, count on your heart to weep about its sadness of being torn apart from that which it once claimed. Use these banners of love as a cue: When you see someone suffering from a broken heart, allow your love to comfort, support and strengthen their resolve to get through their time of sorrow. Likewise, when you see someone celebrating their love, generously offer heartfelt congratulations. How and what is your heart feeling? What message is on its banner in the sky for all to see?

Taste-berry promise for the day: I will write out the message I want to pen on the banner of my heart.

Have a Plan

> *Having a plan for achieving a goal is as important as the goal itself.*

Emily Robinson, 15
A Taste-Berry Teen's Guide to Setting & Achieving Goals

Maybe you want to buy a used car, pass a particular final, save for college, get your parents to agree on a longer curfew, or maybe you have some other objective. While creating a goal is an important first step, desire alone isn't going to bring results. You need a strategy, a carefully laid plan to bring about your desired outcome. Without a plan, you run the risk of letting things happen randomly, by chance or by accident. And if you just go along letting life happen at will, randomly, you never know how things will turn out. Maybe it will be just fine, and you'll be happy with any outcome, but maybe it will not be to your liking, and you'll feel disappointed. Probably you've heard any number of people say, "If only I had. . . ." Don't let yourself get caught in the "shoulda, coulda, woulda" category. Having a plan is the key to getting results. What are your goals, and what is your plan for reaching them?

Taste-berry promise for the day: I will write out my plans for achieving my goals.

Live Up to Your Ideals

Confronting your values up close is sometimes rewarding and at other times a bit unsettling. Be courageous and stand guard.

Bettie B. Youngs
Taste Berries for Teens #3

You know someone who is always making mean-spirited—albeit witty—comments about others. You find yourself laughing at her jabs, sometimes even throwing in a dig of your own. Yet each time, there's a voice that whispers, "This isn't 'nice.' You shouldn't do it." And you feel unsettled as your conscience reminds you that you're not living up to your highest ideals. Perhaps, you've refrained from adding your own digs. Maybe you've even found the courage to point out something positive to counter the mean-spirited comments. If so, you probably experienced a sense of satisfaction for being courageous and living up to your ideals. It can be both "rewarding" and "unsettling" to recognize how and where you are succeeding or falling short. Stand guard over your values: Identify, admit and accept when you are off course—when you have strayed from your values. This "guarding" is how we become a better, wiser and more courageous person.

Taste-berry promise for the day: I will inventory just how I lived up to my values today.

Be Creative

*M*aking the decision to be a "possibilities thinker" has changed my entire way of seeing—and doing—things.

Christopher Lee Byrd
Taste Berries for Teens #3

When you hear "we need creative minds," do you feel intimidated, thinking you're just not creative? Well, the truth is that you are creative by your very nature. Your choices play a part in creating your realities—for better or for worse—each and every day. Take the time to think of the possibilities: What kind of realities would you like to create for yourself and for your world? Your choices—the words, actions and attitudes you choose—really do matter. And your possibilities for creating good are limitless! Choose wisely.

Taste-berry promise for the day: I will consider the realities I would like to create for my life.

Focus on the Moment at Hand

*W*hen I'm feeling stressed, I bear down and focus on
what's in front of me, asking, "What has to get
done right now, right here, right this very second?"

Mitch Reneir, 17
A Taste-Berry Teen's Guide to Setting & Achieving Goals

Sometimes you can end up feeling as if there aren't enough hours in the day to accomplish everything you need to get done. A matter-of-fact approach helps: What is most worth doing? What needs to be done right now to make it most successfully through this moment? What can wait? Make a daily "to-do" list, then learn a "first things first" method. Concentrating and working on the moment at hand is a good way to make it through the immediate stress. When you do this, it moves you to action. Otherwise, you may get paralyzed by "overwhelm" and do nothing. Don't forget to plan ahead so that you're not always caught in the jaws of stress. Learn to use your time wisely: Practice "first things first" and plan ahead.

Taste-berry promise for the day: I will make a "to-do" list of all my activities for the day and use it to get through them.

Listen to the Voice Inside

Your soul has an innate wisdom. Always it knows what it needs. Listen carefully.

Bettie B. Youngs
Taste Berries for Teens

When you face major problems or big decisions, stop and listen. For example, you feel as if a friendship or dating someone isn't good for you anymore. Still, you wonder whether or not this is so, and besides, what should you do about these feelings? Take the time to listen to the voice as it whispers from within. When you're confused or could use some encouragement and direction, stop and listen. Trust that the answers are already within you, "answers" that can support and guide you. But remember, these are yours only when you are willing to be still enough to listen carefully to that wisdom.

Taste-berry promise for the day: I will pay attention to my inner wisdom.

Take Care of the Earth

It was seeing how small our planet appeared in the very vastness of this universe that filled me with the greatest sense of love for it.

Steve Smith, astronaut
Taste Berries for Teens

Our planet, the home we all share, is filled with beauty and everything we need to sustain us, if we just care for it. We can sometimes forget that it is possible for it to run out of certain resources. We are wise to practice conservation. We can sometimes forget how fragile and vulnerable our Earth home is. When not in ecological balance, it may not be able to care for its inhabitants. We must both care *about* it and care *for* it. Don't forget to be a taste berry to the planet.

Taste-berry promise for the day: I'll list five ways I do my part in caring for my Earth home.

Use Your Words Wisely

*W*ords are very powerful. . . . While they may not break your bones, they can break your heart.

Audrianne Adams, 16
More Taste Berries for Teens

It's so important to remember the power of our words—they are not to be taken lightly. A thoughtless remark has the potential to wound someone's heart. The momentary satisfaction you might find in venting cannot compare to the hurt feelings you could inflict. On the other hand, your words also have the capacity to soothe, comfort, build up, support, guide and help others. They can inspire love, hope and faith. Be a taste berry: Use your words to heal and create good feelings.

Taste-berry promise for the day: I will say something kind or helpful to each person I spend time with today.

Share Your Secrets

*B*ringing your "secrets" out into the open means the
truth is no longer hidden. The shame you feel is let
out of its deep and dark cage and so finally you are "freed."

Tina Moreno
A Teen's Guide to Living Drug-Free

Are you harboring any secrets? Do you know something that
no one else knows? Have you done something for which you're
truly ashamed? Keeping past mistakes a secret allows them to
grow and fester in shame. It has been said that secrets grow in
the dark and die in the light. When you share deep-seated hurts
and pains with someone you can trust, it takes some of the
power out of the shame so that you can let go of it and get on
with your life. Have the courage to bring your secrets into the
light and "let them go." Then be a taste berry: Make it safe for
someone else to let go of her secrets, too.

Taste-berry promise for the day: I will share a
"secret" with someone I trust.

Find the Purpose in Your Life

Even though I haven't exactly discovered it yet, I know my life has some really great purpose. I just feel it inside.

David Samson, 18
More Taste Berries for Teens

Have you ever felt the excitement of working on a new project? Have you felt the thrill of doing something that you feel really good or motivated about? Have you experienced the enthusiasm of having some goal or purpose for which you know you are meant to aim? Perhaps you want to help clean up the beaches or the fields in your area. Maybe there's a mural you'd like to help paint as part of a community beautification project. Maybe you are looking at your future, right now! Feeling purpose is about the inspiration to create greater good and beauty in the world each day. Stay open to the call to find great purpose in your life. And don't forget to check to see if it's already arrived!

Taste-berry promise for the day: I will make a list of five things that make me feel purposeful.

Good Listeners Make Good Friends

When you listen to someone—without judging—you free that person to explore deeper levels of their own truth.

Jennifer Leigh Youngs
Taste Berries for Teens

It's said that we have two ears and only one mouth—for a reason. We are meant to listen twice as much as we talk. Do you feel like you're a "good listener"? Would others readily agree with your assessment? When you truly listen to someone, without judging, the other person feels heard—in a word, valued. This is why those who are good listeners are often sought out as friends. Listening connects you to the other person and encourages trust. How do you show that you are a good listener? Give your full attention when someone is talking. Look at that person, show your interest and suspend all judgment. Be a taste berry: Simply listen with an open heart.

Taste-berry promise for the day: I will practice giving my full attention and being a good listener.

Be a Peacekeeper

he ability to set aside the need to be right is a sign of a generous heart.

Bettie B. Youngs
Taste Berries for Teens #3

Has someone ever been "more right" than you, but let it slide—not saying anything, not even "I told you so"? If so, no doubt you found their gesture very gracious! When you can forgo the ego's satisfaction in making someone else wrong so that you can prove that you're right, you are acting from a deeper part of yourself—from a space of love and kindness. Rather than prolonging or creating conflict or animosity, you are choosing to be a peacekeeper on your corner of the planet. When you're in the midst of a disagreement and you choose to listen and seek understanding, you give the other person permission to act from their highest stance of understanding, as well. Allowing human kindness to claim the victory is the mark of a wise and true taste berry.

Taste-berry promise for the day: I will try and understand what the other person is feeling when I'm in a disagreement.

Honesty Makes You Feel Good

I'd rather fail a test honestly, than pass one at the price of cheating for the simple reason that cheating just isn't worth the way it makes me feel about myself.

Les Williamson, 16
Taste Berries for Teens

Have you ever gotten yourself in trouble by telling the truth? For example, did you admit you had your friends over once when you were baby-sitting, when you knew you weren't supposed to? Even though there may have been consequences, didn't you still feel good about yourself for being honest? Always act with integrity. Integrity is about being right with yourself. Strive always to be aligned with what you profess to be your highest and your best. This is one way to experience the satisfaction that comes from knowing you're a winner at life—no matter what. Don't cheat yourself out of this most noble victory. If you do, your self-esteem will suffer, and then you'll have to repair the damage to your wounded sense of self. Instead, just do it right from the get-go: Be honest.

Taste-berry promise for the day: I will journal about the satisfaction I feel when I am honest and act with integrity.

Have Diverse Friends

Having all sorts of friends, especially those with different tastes and preferences, can mean getting to try both pizza and sushi, rock and hip-hop, cardigans and sweats.

Sarah Erdmann, 15
A Taste-Berry Teen's Guide to Setting & Achieving Goals

Oftentimes, you may be drawn to friends who are most like you—who dress like you, share your interests and tastes in music, food and ideas for fun. Having friends with so much in common is just great! But keep an open mind when it comes to building friendships. Think diversity: Be open to the possibility of friends who have different tastes and preferences from you. Enjoying friends with ethnic, racial and religious backgrounds different than your own can mean a new glimpse of and appreciation for different cultures, customs and philosophies. Having diverse friends gives you the benefit of a whole new read on the world—and your place within it. Remain open to a diversity of friends and marvel at how their differences add more to your life.

Taste-berry promise for the day: I will ask my friends to tell me about their culture so that we can discuss our diversities.

Get Some Sleep!

You are your body's guardian: It is totally dependent upon you to take care of it. Start with a good night's sleep.

Jennifer Leigh Youngs
Feeling Great, Looking Hot & Loving Yourself! Health, Fitness and Beauty for Teens

Do you always have a "ton" of homework just waiting for you to make the time to get it done? Do you never seem to have all the time you'd like to be with family and friends—and still have some left over for a little alone time for yourself? Do you get to practice on time and still manage to complete your chores? Chances are you have an exciting, hectic and activity-filled life. One of the best ways to meet all that you have to do is to be sure you're spending enough hours . . . sleeping! That's right. *Sleep is your body's recovery period.* Sleep rejuvenates you and assures that you are up to meeting your schedule, day after day. In fact, health experts say that teens need to get ten to twelve hours of sleep each night just to maintain their intense stage of growth and development. Make sure you're taking good care of yourself by getting the sleep you need each night so that your body is able to meet the daily demands of your life. Be your body's taste berry: Be its faithful guardian.

Taste-berry promise for the day: I will go to bed in time to get the sleep I need each night.

Discover Who You Are

I need to be *"who I am."*

Chad Dalton, 16
Taste Berries for Teens

Part of being "who I am" is discovering "who I am not." For example, maybe you go out for soccer, and then discover that you would rather spend your "sports" time running or cycling. Looking a little closer, perhaps you discover you're a person who prefers one-on-one or noncompetitive sports instead of "team" sports—or maybe the opposite is true. Perhaps you've found yourself doing things or being in situations that didn't feel right. At such times, you just know this is not "who I am." You are then able to move on to things that do feel right. Be open to trying new things (so long as they don't compromise your values) and listen to how you're "feeling and faring" as you go for it. Becoming "who you are" is the work of life. Self-discovery is an important part of the journey, so stay on course!

Taste-berry promise for the day: I will journal on when I found myself in situations that didn't feel right.

Who Can You Turn To?

When my world gets confusing, frightening, even maddening, I find myself looking to someone who can help me feel grounded. Feeling secure, I've learned, is about having "anchors" in my life.

Jennifer Leigh Youngs
A Taste-Berry Teen's Guide to Managing the Stress and Pressures of Life

Even in the best of times, we need people in our lives who we can talk to about our feelings and our lives. When you feel afraid of the world or unsure of yourself, who do you talk with about these matters? Who do you turn to, to discuss your feelings and fears? Whoever you identified is a taste berry for sure. Be certain to let this person know that you value and honor being able to turn to her. Take the time to remind this person how her being there for you helps you feel grounded. Let her know that her presence in your life is a safe place where you can let go of any pretense of feeling brave and strong when you're feeling overwhelmed, hurt or out of sorts.

Taste-berry promise for the day: I will list two people who I can turn to when I'm uncertain about something and thank them for being there for me.

See the Good in Others

Be known as a person who creates harmony.

Patricia Hill Burnett
Feeling Great, Looking Hot & Loving Yourself! Health, Fitness and Beauty for Teens

Have you ever spent time with someone who was content with life, with herself and with others? Someone who helped you feel safe and secure? How do you create such harmony? See the good in others. It's an easy thing to do: If you notice a friend or classmate who is in an especially good mood, you can say, "Being in a good mood sure looks great on you!" If someone is having a bad day, stop and listen. Show empathy. It just might be the response needed to keep "overwhelm" from happening. Create harmony: Be a taste berry who encourages others to feel good about themselves.

Taste-berry promise for the day: I will help others feel good about themselves.

Silence Your Self-Critic

reat yourself with respect. Don't belittle or put yourself down.

Jeanie Metcalf, 15
More Taste Berries for Teens

We all have an inner voice talking to us all the time. Often the voice is there to encourage you, to cheer you on, whispering things such as: "Come on! You can do it! Go for it! You're a winner! Don't give up!" And other times this voice takes on the role of a critic, creating self-doubt and causing you to second-guess yourself, saying things like, "Are you sure you can do this? There's no way you can! Why bother—just give up!" Either way, cheerleader or harsh critic, you know the subtle but real impact of these suggestions. It matters what you tell yourself: The positive inspires you while the negative holds you back. The good news is that just as training and exercise make your muscles strong, you can coach your inner voice to "pump up" the volume on words that are positive and constructive. Start this exercise by reminding that voice of its goal—which is to help you do better and be better—always.

Taste-berry promise for the day: I will look in the mirror and tell myself two ways that I am a winner.

Turn Negatives into Positives

ome very good lessons come from mistakes—even though it doesn't feel like it when in the middle of them.

Helena Moreno, 18
Taste Berries for Teens

Even a negative, like a mistake, can be turned into a positive, like a lesson learned. If you're late for class and end up getting detention, chances are you'll make a better effort to get to class on time. If you repeat a rumor and are confronted about it, you'll probably think twice about gossiping again. If you give your heart too quickly in a romance and it gets taken for granted, or worse, broken as a result, you'll do things differently the next time around. Some of life's important lessons come at the expense of having made a mistake. So when you've erred, forgive yourself and look to the lesson. The goal is to use what you've learned to do better and be better the next time around.

Taste-berry promise for the day: I will journal about the lessons I learned from a recent mistake.

Let Go

*ometimes you have to pick up your heart and go
on—alone.*

Jennifer Leigh Youngs
Taste Berries for Teens Journal

Have you ever had a friend who wasn't good for you—perhaps because he or she influenced you to do things, say things or be someone other than you know yourself to be? Have you ever been in love with a special someone but knew the relationship wasn't right for you? When things aren't right, you need to "let go"—with love. Yes, this can be difficult to do, especially if your heart isn't quite yet ready to be without the other person. Even so, sometimes you have to pick up your heart and go home. You don't have to make the other person "wrong" or "bad" so that you seem justified in "letting go." Let go because you know it's right for you—and because you love and honor yourself enough to know this. Even if the other person doesn't want out of the relationship and asks why you are leaving, rather than saying, "Because you don't/can't/won't . . ." and so on, simply say, "I need to leave because this is not right for me." Letting go can be something you do as a way to love your own heart—because you hold it in the highest regard.

Taste-berry promise for the day: I will journal about what's good—and not so good—about the relationships I share with others.

Confession Is Good for the Soul

"Fess up when you mess up" is the surest way to not have others lose trust in you!

Rae Cheng, 15
More Taste Berries for Teens

Admitting when you are wrong or when you've made a mistake is a mark of true character. It can be tempting to want to ignore your mistake or cover it up, but when you accept responsibility for it, and apologize and right the wrong to the best of your ability, then you have the reward of feeling better about yourself. Admitting your mistakes and errors, and then making amends, builds self-respect. The more you do this, the easier it is to do it gracefully, and without feeling embarrassed or like a failure. Take the first step toward reclaiming your standing as a success: "Fess up" when you make a mistake.

Taste-berry promise for the day: I will admit when I've made a mistake—and make amends.

Be Honest with Yourself

Even if no one else finds out what you've done, you know, and in the end, that's who matters most.

Tomoko Ogata, 15
Taste Berries for Teens

You see someone drop money without being aware of it. You could let the person know about it, or you could pick up the money and slip it into your pocket—maybe no one but you would ever know. Yet that "but you" is the clincher: YOU WOULD KNOW! As the saying goes, *"No matter where you go, there you are!"* Think about it: No matter where you go on your journey through life—no matter where you may end up on this planet—there you are! Being a "good person" who is honest and does what is right makes you a welcome presence to the traveling companion you'll always have along: you. And, of course, being an honest person also makes the trip more enjoyable for others you meet along the way.

Taste-berry promise for the day: I will list three ways I could be even more honest with myself.

Treasure Love's Keepsakes

*ove makes a treasure out of any gift given in its
name.*

Elmer Adrian
Taste Berries for Teens

A single wildflower plucked spontaneously and handed to
you as a gesture of kindness or love; a funny-looking stuffed animal; a comical card; a sappy poem; a mushy note; a goofy drawing—any of these given in the name of love are bound to become
a keepsake to the person to whom they are given. Do you have a
drawer of treasures you cherish—those tokens that remind you
of the love with which they were given? Hopefully, you do!
Treasure these testaments of love's power to remind us that so
little can mean so much. And on those days when you're feeling
a little less than loved, look over your keepsakes—they'll remind
you that you're a loveable person.

Taste-berry promise for the day: I will create a treasure chest especially for the tokens of love I've been given—and
those to come.

Day 132

Choose Your Battles

Is fighting over what you're fighting over worth fighting over?

Nick Barry, 17
Taste Berries for Teens

You've probably heard the saying, "Pick your battles carefully." Have you ever had an argument with your mom or dad or brother or sister or best friend or a special someone, and later thought, *Was that really worth it?* Oftentimes, it really wasn't; you simply got caught up in trying to prove a point that in the end didn't really matter. In fact, the price of the conflict far outweighed any benefit you might've gained. Of course, there are other times when you do need to stand up for yourself or some cause you are defending. When the time comes for you to say, "No, this isn't right," or, "I won't allow you to treat me that way," it should be based on taking care of yourself and siding with your own integrity. These times call for strong, clear communication, not violence, bullying or harsh words. This means being assertive, not being aggressive. Even standing up for yourself should be done with respect for others. Be a taste berry at all times, even in times of conflict.

Taste-berry promise for the day: I will practice saying, "No, that is not all right with me," out loud several times today.

High Goals Are Achievable

Set your goals high and never give in . . . and never give up!

Steve Smith, astronaut
Taste Berries for Teens

Do you remember learning to ride a bike—all the wobbling and spills? Probably you just kept getting up and getting back on the bike until you didn't wobble or fall anymore. The same applies to achieving your goals. Let's say you want to be a veterinarian; that's your goal—you're aiming high. Now come some realities: It's a lot of years of expensive schooling, and you don't know where you are going to come up with the money, to say nothing of those two years when you didn't take school seriously and got low grades. You know it's time to get going. From summer school to part-time jobs, from signing up for that trig class after all to getting some stellar grades, you have much work to do. Most goals are like this: In the beginning, there will be times when you feel "wobbly," and you may even fail. Do not get discouraged. Just as you no doubt eventually learned to sail down the street on your bike, if you never give in and never give up, you will be successful in reaching your goals.

Taste-berry promise for the day: I will discuss my goals with my parents and take suggestions for how to avoid getting discouraged by setbacks in reaching them.

Work Through Grief

Grieving knows no time line. Expect that you will feel many different emotions; allow yourself the freedom of expressing these feelings without judging them.

Bettie B. Youngs
Taste Berries for Teens #3

Grief is our body's way of telling us how beautifully human it is that our hearts can care about another human being so much that we actually hurt when we are without the fellowship and companionship of that special person. Until your grief eases, which it will in its time, practice courage in the day, even though your heart is hurting. Always choose to do what is best for you, which may well include seeking help in working through your grief. Celebrate the passing of your pain. In time, and with the love, support and understanding of family and friends, your feelings of pain will subside, and the wonderful and positive memories of the relationship you shared will be the ones you remember most. Remember, grieving is not about forgetting. It is about expressing being human—which includes the gift of feeling all of the things you do.

Taste-berry promise for the day: I will write a letter of good-bye to someone or something I have lost.

Friends Are Like Mirrors

riends are the very best mirrors we have.

Bettie B. Youngs
More Taste Berries for Teens

Have you ever had a friend say you looked great at a moment when you were feeling like you looked geeky? Has a friend ever been there to tell you how well you did at something—like a speech or sport or even talking to someone you had a crush on—right when you thought you had totally blown it? Didn't it feel just great to have someone see you as a winner when your own view of things was so much less bright? Good friends are like that—always looking at you with hopeful eyes. Never is this a greater gift than when you're being hard on yourself. Be sure to take notes: Good friends can model how you can be a friend to yourself.

Taste-berry promise for the day: I will tell a friend how well he or she did at something.

How Do You Envision the World?

One act, one word, one person and one day at a time . . . make a positive difference in the world.

Jennifer Leigh Youngs
Taste Berries for Teens

What are your highest dreams and visions of our world? Do you see it as a place where the rich resources of our planet are protected and nurtured—beginning with mankind? Do you behold brotherhood, a world without wars, where every nation lives in peace? Does the vision include neighborhoods and communities that are free of violence, where all people genuinely care for each other? Is it a dream of a world that is without hunger or poverty? Do you sometimes feel as if your vision is so grand and the needs so great that you don't know where to begin to create it? The place to begin is right where you are, making a difference in whatever ways you can, to each person you can, one day at a time, one person at a time. Never doubt your ability to make a difference: Singular acts, done for one person at time, in this one single day of your life are able to make a positive difference in the world.

Taste-berry promise for the day: I will make an effort to be friendly to someone who is shy and doesn't have a lot of friends.

Friends Help You Know Yourself

A friend is someone with whom I can reveal the many parts of me, even those I am meeting for the first time.

Jennifer Leigh Youngs
Taste Berries for Teens

Are you often surprised by the way you feel? Do the things you think and say sometimes come as a huge surprise to you? You're always learning, growing and changing. So much is going on that it can sometimes feel like even you can't keep track of "who" you really are. Luckily, friends—especially those who make it safe for you to be yourself—can help you get to know each new facet of you as it unfolds and comes to life. As they are there to listen and talk things over with you, they make it easier for you to become better acquainted with these new parts of yourself. This is one more reason for making sure that you choose to be with those who are positive people, those who feel secure in and of themselves. Seek out taste-berry friends.

Taste-berry promise for the day: I will thank a good friend for allowing me the space to grow and change.

Day 138

Things Have a Way of Working Out

Life's challenges don't always have instant solutions. More times than not, overcoming challenges takes waiting things out.

Trey Oberg, 16
A Teen's Guide to Living Drug-Free

Have you ever had a problem and panicked because you just didn't know what to do, only to later find that the problem took care of itself? Hopefully, you were able to restore your cool before you reacted in ways that only made things worse. When faced with challenges, keep an open mind when looking at solutions—one of which may be "waiting things out." Sometimes moving forward on your journey through life takes standing still for a moment, practicing patience and waiting things out. Learn to allow for the possibility that sometimes "doing nothing" may be the right thing to do.

Taste-berry promise for the day: I will be a patient person today.

Learn from Difficult Experiences

If you've weathered a difficult time, look for the ways you've become stronger and wiser.

Bettie B. Youngs
Taste Berries for Teens

Have you ever broken off a friendship with a special someone and thought you'd never fall in love again? When the next special someone came along, didn't you learn that when love ends, the world doesn't? Didn't this knowledge make you stronger and wiser? Perhaps you thought you'd never be able to make new friends if your parents moved the family to a new city, only to find yourself in no time with a whole new set of friends at your new school. Each difficult experience in our lives can help us become wiser—if we so choose. When faced with a challenge, ask yourself, "What can I learn from this?" "What new perspective has this situation given me?" Take the treasure of this new perspective and let it be a great consolation prize, turning what may once have looked like a loss into a winning "jackpot" in your life.

Taste-berry promise for the day: I will talk to a friend about the ways a difficult time helped me gain a better perspective.

Find an Anchor

Knowing that I can share my concerns and insecurities helps me feel more stable in a constantly changing world. As a result, I am more at peace and complete within myself.

Jennifer Leigh Youngs
Taste Berries for Teens #3

The power of having someone in our lives whose love remains the same in spite of the changes in the world and the changes in ourselves is one of the most amazing sources of security. It is this kind of "rock" or "anchor" in our lives—often a parent or grandparent—who helps us rest in the peaceful waters of knowing we are loved and accepted come what may, when we might otherwise be tossed about by the turbulent storms of change. It is natural to be grateful for these anchors in our lives. Who are the people who make you feel secure? Thank them for helping you feel safe at a time in your life when both you and the world around you are rapidly changing.

Taste-berry promise for the day: I will tell the three people who make me feel most "stable" how much their love and support mean to me.

Accept Yourself

To be accepted by others and to feel as if we belong support our natural instincts for self-acceptance.

Bettie B. Youngs
More Taste Berries for Teens

It's the first day of school, and the halls seem filled with kids you don't know. Suddenly, you spot a circle of your friends—instantly you relax as you walk over to join them, as they smile and greet you. When we feel accepted by others, we're more accepting of ourselves. It's nice to know that you can give this gift of acceptance to others, as well. When we are brought into the "fold" of a group of caring people—whether friends or family—we feel part of something bigger. This experience of belonging helps us move beyond the fear of rejection to become more ourselves and to share more of who we are with the world. Strive daily to accept others and yourself in this way.

Taste-berry promise for the day: I will invite someone who looks lonely to sit with my friends and me at lunch.

Happiness Is the Best Success

Being happy with yourself is the starting point for being a successful human being.

Bettie B. Youngs
More Taste Berries for Teens

What is your definition of a successful human being? Is it the person who is really popular on campus—the star of the football team or the head cheerleader? Perhaps you think it's the person who has great friends, the one who everyone thinks is "a really nice person." Is your definition of success the student who always gets good grades? Or is it the person who has all the right clothes and the coolest "things"? It's good to think about your definition of success so that you'll know when you're experiencing it. Success begins with being happy with yourself. Without this happiness, your successes may feel empty: Do you know someone who seems to have many triumphs and victories and is still unhappy? The best success in life is being a happy human being—which depends on being happy with yourself.

Taste-berry promise for the day: I will make a list of all the ways I am happy with myself.

Our Global Family

We are a global family; we are all responsible for each other, as well as for the planet we share.

Jennifer Leigh Youngs
Taste Berries for Teens Journal

Take time to reflect on how you are part of a global family. It's easy to get wrapped up in your own day-to-day life, getting along at home and making it through school and social obligations. The thought of being part of a national family, let alone a global family, is the farthest thing from your mind. But forgetting doesn't make it any less true—it only diminishes your ability to stand up and be counted as a responsible member of "the family." Kindness and service are the actions that assure you are doing your part. They are more than just "quick heart-warmers"; they are your responsibility and your honor. Look for ways you can be of service to others.

Taste-berry promise for the day: I will list two ways that I am being a responsible member of my global family.

Show Love to Your Family

Each family develops its own "language," its own way to show love, affection and connection.

Marcus Lamont, 17
A Teen's Guide to Living Drug-Free

When was the last time you told each member in your family that you loved them? Because we see our family members every day, and know that we're going to see them again and again each day—because we count on them being there—it's easy to take our relationships with them for granted. But we shouldn't. Instead, we should shower as much love and support on each of our family members as we can. These human beings—who providence has placed in your life—can provide you with some of your greatest lessons in loving, patience, forgiveness and acceptance. Setting aside expectations of the "storybook" family, embrace and appreciate the "language" your family has developed for showing love, affection and connection. Don't forget to do all you can to help each of your family members feel loved and accepted. This is how a family grows "healthy."

Taste-berry promise for the day: I will do something special to share my love with each member of my family.

You Are One of a Kind

*J*ust like every flower is beautiful in its own way, being
an individual bloom is wonderful for people, too.

Alana Ballen, 13
Taste Berries for Teens

Do you ever look at other people and wish you were more like
them? Do you ever wish you were taller, shorter, funnier,
smarter, like this person or that person? It's not unusual to want
to be like everyone else—to fear being "different" in some way.
But it's simply not wise to compare yourself with others. Have
you ever looked at the blossom of a single flower in a vase? As it
rested atop the pedestal of its elegant stem, weren't the colorful
plumes of its petals gorgeous? Its solitary beauty would not have
been so striking if it were placed in a huge bouquet of other flowers. You, too, are more radiant as a one of a kind. Who you are is
your individuality—although part of a larger whole, it's your
own unique individual qualities that represent your personal
petals of beauty and appeal. Appreciate your own beauty. Feel
confident being in a "vase" of your very own.

Taste-berry promise for the day: I will consider all the
ways I've grown better and become more "me" over the past
year.

Seek Out Your Successes

The more success you experience, the less likely it is that you will feel devastated or deflated by periodic setbacks.

Bettie B. Youngs
More Taste Berries for Teens

Did you make it to all of your classes on time? Did you get all of your homework done? Did you hit a home run or increase your speed in track? Look for your successes; they are there in each day. Perhaps there was a fashion statement you pulled together perfectly, or maybe you were there to help a friend. There's success to be found at school, at home and in your social life. Acknowledge and congratulate yourself for your triumphs and achievements. Developing the eyes and attitudes that pick up on what it is you're succeeding at will help you get through those times when you experience a failure or meet up with an obstacle you can't quite overcome. By noting when and how you succeed, you'll soon build a storehouse of positive experiences. On those days when things simply do not go as planned, compare your "off" day with the storehouse of your track record of successes. It's sure to make the failures less devastating.

Taste-berry promise for the day: I will look in the mirror and congratulate myself for my latest success.

Make a Dream Map

See it! Believe it! Achieve it!

Jennifer Leigh Youngs
A Taste-Berry Teen's Guide to Setting & Achieving Goals

Setting your goals and then focusing on doing those things required to make them happen is what changes those goals into accomplishments. First identify and prioritize your goals, then chart them out in daily, weekly and monthly "to-do's." Each of these steps is important; each moves you closer to your goals, and makes it easier for you to see what you need to do to achieve them. Create a definite destination that you can see in your mind's eye as you set out to make each of your goals happen. You can even make a "dream map" for yourself, some visual reminder of what your goal is—like a picture you hang in your room or a poster board of written reminders of where you are going. This "map" is your cheerleader encouraging you to meet your dreams. When you have your goals in front of you, you can more clearly see when you're on or off course. What's most important is to maintain your attitude for success: See your goals as possible and believe in your ability to achieve them. Do what it takes to own this attitude.

Taste-berry promise for the day: I will create a "visual reminder" of my goal and place it where it can cheer me on.

Keep an Open Mind

Minds are like parachutes; they won't work unless they're open.

Jennifer Leigh Youngs
A Teen's Guide to Living Drug-Free

What's the use of a parachute that won't open? It allows for only one possibility—and not a very bright one at that. So keep your mind in working order—keep it open. How can you have a broader vision of life if you refuse to raise your eyes and look at a new horizon? How can you hear new ideas if you don't listen to them? You are a student of life: Open your mind to a world of greater wisdom, knowledge and new ideas. Read broadly, have discussions about current events with interesting and diverse friends, watch educational programs, open yourself to others who are bright, "with it" and who you know have "sage" advice. When you do these things, your mind stays open—and you're sure to land safely as the winds of life take you into a world of greater possibilities.

Taste-berry promise for the day: I will discuss current events with my friends.

Have Something to Look Forward To

*T*he source of confidence, motivation, sass, spunk and
vitality—all traits that give a person "presence"—
comes from feeling purposeful.

Jennifer Leigh Youngs
Feeling Great, Looking Hot & Loving Yourself! Health, Fitness and Beauty for Teens

Do you admire how some of your friends have a real dynamic
"attitude" or a cool confidence, and they're not afraid to speak
their minds and try new things? Isn't it great how some friends
just seem to have lives that are exciting and interesting? Want to
know the secret to possessing these traits? It's a simple one:
Have something important that you're looking forward to and
working toward. Owning such purpose is the birthplace for the
inner qualities of zest and zeal. Pursuing goals that are important to you gives meaning to your life. You, too, can be a powerful presence: Discover those goals that give your life purpose
and then set out to achieve them with the passion they inspire.

Taste-berry promise for the day: I will talk to my parents about goals that could help me feel purposeful.

Watch for Synchronicity

If we watch closely, and most especially if we are looking for it, we will find that synchronicities happen in our lives quite frequently.

Bettie B. Youngs
Taste Berries for Teens

What is synchronicity? Synchronicity is a word used to describe a meaningful coincidence of two or more events where something other than the probability of chance is involved. It is almost as if something has been orchestrated by divine intervention. Remember those times when one surprise was followed by another surprise, then followed by another? Whether you called it luck, good fortune or just "really weird," wasn't it magical to know that there was something greater at work in your world? If you look for these "coincidences," you're sure to see them everywhere. Where are those synchronicities around you? Allow them to add a dash of wonder to your life.

Taste-berry promise for the day: I will write a story about a time when a synchronicity occurred in my life.

Dream Big

*𝒥 was an ambitious kid with a wild, wild imagination.
Not too much has changed except that I've turned my
wild imagination into my greatest ambition, set goals
around it, and now my "imagine ifs" are no longer beyond
my wildest imagination!*

Thomas Hatfield, 16
A Taste-Berry Teen's Guide to Setting & Achieving Goals

Do you want to backpack through Europe? Climb Mt.
Everest? Find a cure for AIDS? Create safe playgrounds throughout your community to keep kids off the streets? You can do
great things—so be sure to dream big. What "mechanism" do
you use to stimulate your (wild) imagination—to "think big"?
Do you hang around with creative friends who themselves have
big plans for their lives? Do you read broadly, exposing yourself
to great minds and great ideas to help expand your own sense of
things? Do you attend classes and lectures to motivate your
"ambition"? Do you watch TV shows and films that are interesting and educational? Do you observe others as they go about
their lives, evaluating if what you see is something you'd like to
emulate or expand upon? Of course these are not the only ways
to "motivate your imagination," but the point is, your dreams
become your goals. So think big and dream big: The world is
waiting for the taste berry you offer.

Taste-berry promise for the day: I will check out one
of the classics at the library and begin to read it.

151

You Can Do It!

You gain confidence and grow more resilient each time you work through and overcome a tough time.

Bettie B. Youngs
Taste Berries for Teens

When you make it through a big exam, a job interview, a speech in front of the entire student body or a really big upset with a friend, you probably feel relieved—and thankful—that you did! The next time a similar challenge comes along, you have the experience of that "first time around" to draw upon. And so you are better able to believe you can make it through this one. And when you make it through yet again, your insecurity lessens, and your confidence grows greater. Again and again, as you face and conquer the hardships in your life, big and small, you become more and more resilient. Trust that no matter how difficult your life may seem, no matter how much turbulence you run into, you can make it through. Focus not on the problem, but rather on your flight.

Taste-berry promise for the day: I will make a list of all the challenges I've victoriously overcome in the past school year.

Live Drug-Free

By staying drug-free, you get a better "read" on your emotions and the reasons behind them, whether joy, sorrow or pain.

Jennifer Leigh Youngs
A Teen's Guide to Living Drug-Free

Just as an over-the-counter drug like aspirin masks your ability to feel the pain of a headache, alcohol and drugs can mask your ability to think clearly as they cloud and distort your sense of things. There are many prices and tolls to pay for using drugs. One of them is that they disconnect you from reality and hide the truth. By staying drug-free, you have a better chance to engage in life for all it is. This consciousness allows you to use these emotions for all that they are, to better develop your intellect and to discover your talents, aptitudes and interests. These are powerful reasons not to put chemicals into your body. Be a taste berry for life: Don't use drugs, and encourage your friends not to use them as well.

Taste-berry promise for the day: I will talk with my friends about all the good reasons not to use drugs.

Time Is a Great Healer

*There is no quick fix to make a heartache go away;
there is much truth to the adage, "It takes time to
heal."*

Bettie B. Youngs
Taste Berries for Teens Journal

The betrayal of a close friend, a breakup with a special someone, the death of a loved one—all can teach us the pain of a
heartache. Certainly in such times we reach out to others to be
consoled and comforted. And yet, we find that not much makes
the pain go away—except for time. Maybe this is meant to be:
The meltdown of an aching heart gets our attention and creates
a greater understanding of our vulnerability and humanness.
Such can expand our capacity for understanding, kindness and
compassion for others. And, of course, we do heal. In time, we
find that our pain will ease. And so we are left knowing—and
respecting—that the human heart is amazingly resilient: It does
not wither under the strain of pain. It can "recover"—and in
doing so, we emerge with a greater sense of stamina, perseverance and resilience. What a miraculous outcome. As others go
through heartache, share the comfort of this hope with them.

Taste-berry promise for the day: I will journal about
my heartaches and how I made it through them all.

Be a Courteous Person

> *If we all practice being courteous, if goodwill is our motto, then we can make a really big difference in the world.*

Cara Robinson, 17
Taste Berries for Teens #3

Being courteous implies an understanding that your own desires need not take precedence over everyone else's. Goodwill calls for being friendly, helpful, caring and supportive. Imagine what the world would be like if everyone was benevolent in these ways! What a shift this would create, so many problems would be dissolved and so many heartaches would be soothed. It can be done—we could create this state! When you're a courteous person and claim goodwill as your motto, person by person, family by family, school by school, community by community, the world moves closer to this beautiful—and essential—vision and ideal. Surely your life is filled with opportunities to be a taste berry in this way. Be an ambassador of goodwill. Consider that your official duties—and lifetime term in the role—start today.

Taste-berry promise for the day: I will be an ambassador of goodwill by offering a kind smile and my assistance at home and school.

Friends Look Out for Each Other

A friend is always looking out for you, always making sure that you're happy, too.

Meghan Sauerheber, 16
More Taste Berries for Teens

Do you have a really good friend who is always looking out for you—who is always covering your back, who has nothing but good things to say about you? Doesn't it feel just great? Good friends support each other in these ways. How do you feel when someone asks, "How does that sound to you?" or "Is that okay with you?" or "What do you think about that?" No doubt, it leaves you feeling included, valued and like your needs matter. In real friendship you give back as much as you get. How do you do this? You make sure your friend is happy, too: You ask your friend about what's going on in her life. You help when she needs a hand, you include her in the fun times and confide in her when times are tough. Taste berries look out for their friends. Don't underestimate the power of learning the art of being a good friend: The world could use many more.

Taste-berry promise for the day: I will ask a friend, "Tell me, what is going on in your life?"

Say "I Love You"

"I love you": Three little words—but ones that hold a huge amount of power.

Jennifer Leigh Youngs
Taste Berries for Teens #3

Do you remember the time you found an "I love you" note in your pocket, lunch or locker? Whether from your mom or dad, grandma or a special someone for whom you "have feelings," being reminded that you are loved feels just great! And here's some more good news about the power of the words "I love you": The expression of them even brings great joy for the person who is declaring his or her love! Recall for a moment the glee you felt as you handed your mom (or another special someone) a gift and watched in great anticipation for her to unwrap it. Love: What an incredible emotion. We need only to be in its presence—whether feeling how much we love someone or feeling the joy of being loved—to understand it is both precious and priceless. Honor this knowing.

Taste-berry promise for the day: I will place an "I love you" note where my mom or dad will find it during their day.

Never Give Up

Hang in there, even when the going gets tough. When you persist, your chances for experiencing success are greater.

Mike Siciliano, 18
A Teen's Guide to Managing the Stress and Pressures of Life

Has there ever been a time when you didn't manage success with the first try—but were still successful in the end? Perhaps you didn't pass a test the first time around—but retested with flying colors. Maybe you didn't get on the team the first time you tried out but made it the next time. Aren't you glad you didn't give up? We wouldn't get far in life or reach many worthy goals if we gave up at the first disappointment (or even at the second or third . . .). In spite of the discouragement you feel over a setback, keep on trying, keep on going, keep on reaching. Even if you feel like your efforts are only accomplishing the smallest degree of progress—remember, progress is progress. As long as you are moving forward, you're headed toward success. Sometimes it takes "hanging in there" to savor the sweetness of the taste berry of success.

Taste-berry promise for the day: I will inventory those times it took "hanging tough" in order to reach success.

Day
159

Live in Harmony with Others

e are all interdependent: Just about everything we do is done in concert with others.

Bettie B. Youngs
More Taste Berries for Teens

Cleaning your room with a good friend, going for a picnic or a long walk with a special someone, watching a movie with your family, even working on a special project with a classmate—each of these activities seems more fun when shared. Doing things with others, sharing our lives, is human nature. What a lovely realization. Have you ever been to an excellent concert where all the musicians play brilliantly off each other? The harmony of the music created by their differing instruments is even more beautiful than the great sounds of each individual instrument. So it is with the harmonies and melodies we can create when we "play the music of life" in concert with others—the song can be more beautiful for the chorus of sounds than it would be as a solo. Learn to play "in concert" with those around you.

Taste-berry promise for the day: I will plan a picnic with my friends.

Be a Leader

It takes courage to stand for your beliefs and act according to your values without worrying about how others might judge you. When you do this, you help others find the courage to do the same.

Mandy Martinez, 17
A Teen's Guide to Living Drug-Free

Deciding to be a leader takes courage: It puts you right out there in front, where everyone can take notice. All your attitudes and actions, everything you say and do, are like Web site messages being posted on the global Internet of life. These messages are going out from you all the time. You have no idea how many people may be "signed on" to your "site"; you probably have a much bigger audience than you think! When you "say no" to drugs or alcohol, or speak up against injustice or racism, or stick up for someone who is being unfairly "razzed" at school, your message is being posted for everyone to see. When you stand up for what is right, you inspire others to find the courage to take a stand for their own values—and post their own taste-berry messages of integrity and kindness.

Taste-berry promise for the day: I will practice saying, "I feel that isn't right."

See Yourself as Valuable

Self-esteem is the "price tag" you place on yourself.

Jennifer Leigh Youngs
Feeling Great, Looking Hot & Loving Yourself! Health, Fitness and Beauty for Teens

Have you ever felt like a million bucks? Great self-esteem can make you feel that way. Self-esteem is self-regard; it's how much you cherish and appreciate being you. In a very real way, your self-esteem is the "price tag" you place on yourself. And yet, this price is "visible" for all the world to see. Not only will others know by your self-esteem what you think of yourself, but they will treat you accordingly. Think of it: Don't you treat your "good" pair of shoes a lot more carefully than the "old" ones? It's all about a self-picture: Are you a "markdown" or a valuable commodity? Choose to see yourself as a precious soul.

Taste-berry promise for the day: I will see myself as a precious soul.

Cherish Your Memories

Memories are life's second chance at happiness.

McKenna Jagger, 15
More Taste Berries for Teens

Do you ever think back on those people whom you've loved and cared about but who are no longer in your life? Perhaps you and an old friend have drifted apart; a special someone has moved away; or someone close to you has passed away. Luckily, "out of sight" isn't always "out of mind": They can still live on in your memories. As you remember the good times, the fun, the understanding and friendship felt and shared—as the feelings stir to life all over again—you realize that there are parts of love that cannot be lost at all. Cherish these taste-berry memories— and today's opportunities to build new ones for tomorrow.

Taste-berry promise for the day: I will honor a happy memory by telling a friend all about it.

Be Accountable for Your Words

You're accountable for every single word that comes out of your mouth: Make sure your words reflect your respect for people.

Bettie B. Youngs
More Taste Berries for Teens

Have you ever had someone say something inconsiderate about your friend, a classmate or even a stranger in passing? You clearly knew this was not okay with you—and hopefully, you let the person talking know it as well. You are accountable for the words you speak in response to someone talking poorly about someone else. It's important to let others know when they are crossing one of your personal boundaries. Having this boundary is one way of showing that you are willing to be accountable for your words. By the same token, when someone is encouraging or kind to someone else, it's important to tell that person how much you appreciate his or her actions, since you are also accountable for words of recognition and praise that inspire others to uphold ideals you value. Make certain that your words always reflect your respect for all people.

Taste-berry promise for the day: I will tell someone how much I respect his or her act of kindness to somebody else.

Ponder the Wonders of Life

*W*e live in a world of creation, one where a universal energy permeates all living matter.

Jennifer Leigh Youngs
Feeling Great, Looking Hot & Loving Yourself! Health, Fitness and Beauty for Teens

Have you ever stopped to look at a sunset or star-filled sky to take in the beauties of nature and just marveled at the vastness of creation? These moments are insightful. In these moments, intuitively we are reminded that our heart, mind, body and soul are "one" with something greater—and all is *perfect*. Herein we can grasp the importance of being in harmony with that which is all around us. Always notice subtle, but real changes going on around you. Eavesdrop on the way the universe silently breathes its wonders into life—and in so doing, beckons you to believe in something even more loving than your own being.

Taste-berry promise for the day: I'll pay more attention to the wonders of life all around me.

Decide to Cope

Eventually, we learn that things don't always go as planned, no matter how cool and in control we think we are, but even so, you don't have to let your cool turn to ghoul!

Bettie B. Youngs
A Taste-Berry Teen's Guide to Managing the Stress and Pressures of Life

Isn't it great when everything is unfolding perfectly, going exactly as planned? Everyone loves those days! But in real life, not every day goes as planned. There are those days when everything seemed to go wrong—the shirt you'd planned to wear was missing a button; the store was out of your favorite cereal; the test wasn't on the pages you studied; and then you found out that your best friend couldn't follow through with the plans you'd made for the upcoming weekend! When things don't go as planned—when life throws you a curveball—it can really affect your cool. Still, the decision to stress out, or not to stress out, is yours. Decide to cope. When life dashes your carefully laid plans by creating unexpected twists and turns, regroup and do the best you can with the situation in the moment. This will help assure that your cool doesn't turn to ghoul.

Taste-berry promise for the day: I will not stress out.

You Are a Work in Progress

*T*he sooner you make friends with the face in the mirror, the better.

Melissa Jean Wiley, 16
Taste Berries for Teens #3

One week you are certain you want to go to college, the next you're thinking maybe you'd rather just get a job after you graduate. One week, you think the high court's ruling on the Pledge of Allegiance was a good thing, and the next week you really have your doubts. One week you think you are finally ready to cut and color your hair in the latest pink and spiked style, and the next you've changed your mind—and you're not quite sure if it means you've lost your courage, or that you've come to your senses. The face in the mirror is always changing: You're a work in progress—some parts of you are "totally excellent" while others are still "under construction." Accept this. Becoming your own good friend is about getting to know, understand and appreciate yourself—no matter what stage of construction you're in.

Taste-berry promise for the day: I will look in the mirror and tell myself, "You are totally loveable just the way you are!"

Day 167

Hang Tough in Tough Times

The toughest times call for the fiercest determination. Hang tough!

Jennifer Leigh Youngs
Taste Berries for Teens

Think back on those times when you really had to work your hardest to reach a goal, when it took sheer resolve to keep going. Did you persevere? Chances are, you did. Determination often leads to follow-through, a precursor to success. As the old adage reminds us, "When the going gets tough, the tough get going." Determination is an attitude you can cultivate; it's not a part of your makeup such as your personality. When the going gets tough, it can be as simple as applying yourself to the task at hand, one foot in front of the other, day by day. No matter what obstacles or challenges stand between you and your goals, you can overcome them if only you remain determined and don't give up. Grit is the taste berry that can bring you through the tough times.

Taste-berry promise for the day: I will complete the task at hand right here and now and apply myself to reaching my goal.

Take Responsibility

Take responsibility for your own actions. It's the only way you're ever going to "own" yourself.

Bettie B. Youngs
A Taste-Berry Teen's Guide to Setting & Achieving Goals

You fail an exam: Is your response, "I should've studied harder," or is it, "The teacher always gives tests that are too hard"? And what about when you get an A? Do you say, "I worked hard and it paid off," or do you say, "I got lucky"? Your friend thanks you for bringing her homework assignments when she was out sick. Do you say, "Oh, it was nothing," or do you say, "You're welcome, I'm glad I could be of help"? Coming up with excuses and minimizing your accomplishments are cop-outs: One refuses to accept where you need change; the other refuses to acknowledge where you stand out. No one else is responsible when you excel or fall short, shine or act poorly. Accepting this responsibility is the mark of a person who is willing to be in charge of his life, open to receive the call for change and to receive the praise.

Taste-berry promise for the day: I will take responsibility for all my actions.

Speak Up for Injustice

𝓘've made a vow to always speak up when I see injustice. It's the single most important thing I can do to contribute to living in a peaceful world.

Alexis Bedford, 14
Taste Berries for Teens #3

Many times silence is seen as agreement. If your friends are being unkind to someone else, it's important to let them know that you don't agree with their actions. Likewise, if they're saying and doing positive things, confirm that you appreciate this. Decide on "who" you are, and then use your voice to speak your convictions. Speaking up is standing for something. Speaking up is being counted among those who are willing to make change in our great world. Speaking up is determining to take your place as a true citizen of the world. Especially in today's times, we need everyone who has the courage to lead the way to create peace. Be among the counted.

Taste-berry promise for the day: I will speak up and say I feel it's wrong if I see a friend being unkind to someone else.

Respect Your Parents

I've never met a teen who didn't want his parents' respect. I've never met a parent who didn't hope he was respected by his teenager.

Bettie B. Youngs
Taste Berries for Teens #3

In the teen years it may seem as if you're so busy with your own life outside the home that you're growing farther and farther away from your parents. Yet deep in your heart you no doubt crave a close, approving relationship—filled with respect, honesty and trust, and based on love. Know that your parents crave exactly this same kind of relationship. Perhaps this is the secret of the family: At heart, both parents and teens sincerely want to share a mutual love and respect for each other. Aside from everything that goes on—and in spite of it—earning the respect of each other is the outcome everyone desires the most. Be sure to let your parents know that you respect them. Tell them, of course, but also let it show in all your actions.

Taste-berry promise for the day: I will tell my parents all the ways I respect them.

Don't Make Comparisons

Don't compare yourself with others. Make your measuring stick for judging yourself within.

Jennifer Leigh Youngs
More Taste Berries for Teens

Perhaps some of your classmates or friends are tall, while some are short; some get good grades, while others struggle just to pass; some are outgoing, while still others are shy. Do you compare yourself to them? Hopefully not: Your "assets" are your own and have nothing to do with anyone else. Getting an A on a test isn't any less of a victory because someone else failed; and getting a failing grade isn't the result of someone else's A. Rejoice in your A because it's yours to celebrate and do what it takes to bring up a failing grade because it's your own progress to make. This holds true in every area of your life. The best measuring stick lies within. Only you can answer the question, "Have I done my best?" Are you open to becoming a "better" taste berry? Grow, change, shine, evolve.

Taste-berry promise for the day: I will journal about how I have done my best and how I can grow and do even better.

Be a Good Influence

We all influence each other, for good and bad.

Susan Shrinkle, 15
Taste Berries for Teens

Have you ever been with a group of friends and witnessed one of them do or say something that you found appalling—and yet, no one else seemed bothered, and so you said nothing? Just one voice can turn the tide: Speak up. No doubt you see many things every day that need a clear and positive voice, whether it's to stop the gossip or spreading of rumors, to say "no" to the suggestion of drinking or smoking or using drugs, to declare why "it's not cool" to lie or cheat or steal. Many times, it is the brave action of one person that brings the support of others, until an entire circle of friends rejects a bad idea and embraces a healthier choice. Yes, amazing power and strength can be found in the influence of others: Vow to influence for good.

Taste-berry promise for the day: I will practice saying, "That's not cool," when I feel that it really isn't.

Lonely When You're Not Alone

here's nothing lonelier than feeling lonely in the middle of a crowd.

Desiree Huerta, 15
More Taste Berries for Teens

Everyone wants to feel like they belong—and that they are free to be themselves and accepted for who they are. Most of us have moments when we struggle with feeling out of place. Think back to your feelings on the first day of school, or coming into a new class late, or showing up to a dance or a party before your friends got there, or walking in the cafeteria alone and wondering where to sit: Did you feel insecure, anxious, lonely? How can you ease the discomfort when you find yourself "feeling lonely in the middle of a crowd"? Remind yourself it's okay to have these moments—they pass—and realize nearly everyone has these feelings at times like these. Knowing this can make you feel less alone and give you greater empathy for others who find themselves in these situations, too. Be a "taste berry": Help everyone feel accepted. This can go a long way toward curing loneliness in your school, in your community and in the world.

Taste-berry promise for the day: I will invite someone who looks left out to sit next to me on the bus or in class.

Treat Others Well

elieve in the expression, "What goes around comes around." It's true.

Becky Coldwell, 15
Taste Berries for Teens

When you live by what is known as the "Golden Rule," treating others with the same respect and kindness with which you'd like to be treated, you find the result is usually that others treat you with respect and kindness, too. Of course, this isn't the reason you are good to others, but it is a natural response to it—and a welcome bonus, as well. Treating others with kindness and respect helps you feel good about yourself, your fellow man and life in general. It is the right thing to do, and it instills a sense of both connection and integrity within you. Regardless of whether it comes back to you, trust that your kindness will be sent out into the universe to land just where it's supposed to!

Taste-berry promise for the day: I will offer my assistance to anyone I see in need.

Pain Is a Teacher

ain is your heart's way of telling you it's wounded and calling on you for a couple of Band-Aids and a bowl of taste berries.

Jennifer Leigh Youngs
Taste Berries for Teens

Have you ever had your feelings hurt and pretended you weren't hurt at all? Have you ever been devastated by someone breaking up with you, but acted as if it was no big deal? Have you ever had your heart broken and gone on about your day, refusing to acknowledge anything was wrong? When your heart is in pain, it can be trying to get your attention. The ache can be telling you to take time to look at how this pain was caused and what it came to teach you. There is something to learn in every heartache if you admit to the pain, look for the lessons—and learn something from them. And, of course, just as you care for an injury of any sort, your heart needs tending also—that's why it's called "nursing" a broken heart. The pain of a broken heart can be seen as your chance to come closer to yourself, to hold yourself, to soothe yourself, to be your own taste berry. Open to the necessity of being a conscious presence in your own life.

Taste-berry promise for the day: I will pamper my heart by surrounding myself with people who love me.

Don't Just Survive—Thrive!

Surviving day by day is not my goal. Thriving is!

Josh Henderson, 19
Taste Berries for Teens

Are you surviving or are you thriving? There's a big difference. For example, is your goal to "get through" the school year, or is your goal to absolutely learn everything, from every class, every day? Is your goal to "have friends" or to "have *close* friends"—those you really know, support and trust? Imagine living with expectations on this level. You can! When you do the bare minimum to get by, you are just surviving. When you put all you have into living your life to its fullest, doing your best, setting goals for yourself and doing the footwork to accomplish them, then you are thriving. It's your life, live it to the fullest— live it with zest, zeal, gusto, passion, purpose! Why not go for it! If not now, when?

Taste-berry promise for the day: I will have a "go-for-it" approach to life!

Choose Laughter

*aughter, when it's not forced or mean-spirited, feels
great and can help us love rather than berate ourselves.*

Bettie B. Youngs
More Taste Berries for Teens

Have you ever done something really embarrassing, and later gotten great joy out of laughing about it with your friends? Have your plans ever gone so hopelessly awry that you had two choices: laugh or cry about it? Choosing laughter, didn't you find much of the sense of calamity around it was eased? That's the way it is with laughter—it lightens up the "heavier" sides of life. When you choose humor it can help remind you not to take yourself so seriously and that your dilemma will no doubt pass. Just like love grows when it is shared, so does the joy of laughter. It takes on a life of its own, returning to you when you need it most. Be a taste berry: Share it freely.

Taste-berry promise for the day: I will share my "lighter" views of life and a good laugh with others.

177

Look for the Good in Others

When you're around people who look for the good in others, it naturally brings out the best in you.

Karen Trusdale, 15
Taste Berries for Teens

Think of the people you know who make it clear that they enjoy other people. Don't you just love to be around them? It feels good and safe to be with someone who is looking for what is positive about you—and everyone else as well. It naturally brings out more of your very best. Guess what? Looking for the positive in others also brings out the good in the person doing the looking! Be a taste berry who brings out the best in yourself by looking for the good in others.

Taste-berry promise for the day: I will tell someone I care about all the "best" I see in him or her.

Promote Positive Change

*M*y little brother sometimes puts his hands over his eyes and shouts, "Now you can't see me!" I'm afraid that's what I've been doing with my life.

Teddy Bonaducci, 18
More Taste Berries for Teens

Have you watched someone go out of her way to help someone else—but failed to mention how thoughtful you felt her actions were? Ignoring the opportunity to give praise where it's deserved is one way of putting your hands over your eyes and pretending your inaction can't be seen by anyone else. Have you ever had a friend who behaved rudely, such as going to the front of the line at lunch or the movies—when others have been waiting? Did you fail to show how thoughtless you considered her actions? Covering your eyes to such behavior can make you as "guilty" as the perpetrator. What's more, others see your action or inaction, even when you try to pretend it doesn't really matter. "See" life and circumstance clearly. What you do, or don't do, does matter. Acknowledging someone who deserves praise, calling on someone to right a wrong, is not only a taste-berry thing to do, but shows you are growing up. Keep your eyes open, state your truth, defend your values and promote positive change in your world.

Taste-berry promise for the day: I will praise a friend who has helped someone or suggest an apology to a friend who has been rude to someone else.

Talk About Your Problems

each out to talk about how things are going for you. When you do, you'll find others know what you are talking about—they've been there.

Jennifer Leigh Youngs
Taste Berries for Teens Journal

The more you keep your problems bottled up inside, the more you tend to convince yourself that no one else could possibly understand. This can magnify your pain, as it sweeps you into feelings of isolation and self-pity. The moment you reach out and begin to talk to someone about what you're going through and how you feel, the spell of isolation is broken—and soon enough, the self-pity starts to melt away, too. You find out that other people really do understand—they've been through similar problems and have experienced their own depths of pain. You may even find out your problems don't loom as large as you think they do. Perhaps most importantly, you and the other person are able to work together to find solutions!

Taste-berry promise for the day: I will discuss my problems with someone I trust.

Review Your Life

I've found it can be helpful to "review" your life now and then, just to see if it's time for a good housecleaning.

Jenny Bilicki, 19
More Taste Berries for Teens

It's good to "review" your life from time to time. When you do, you'll find that at times you are quite satisfied with the things you're doing as well as with the way your life is going. And you'll see that other times you need to make some changes, to "clean house." Dusting the nooks and crannies of your life helps you to see if you've stopped living certain morals or gotten off track in standing for certain values—and recommit to them. Don't be afraid to throw open the shutters and curtains to examine the "program" you use to see your life and the way you're living it. Illuminated by the light of honest introspection, you can see more clearly your assumptions, biases and why you feel as you do about things. Does your "house" need cleaning? Is it time for you to take stock of your values, behaviors and beliefs? Soul-searching is the way of a taste berry.

Taste-berry promise for the day: I will use my journal to "review" my life to see if I'm staying true to my values.

Focus on Today

When things get really tense, I find that if I just take care of the day and not worry about tomorrow until tomorrow, then I'll be okay; I can get through it.

Kyla Branson, 16
A Teen's Guide to Living Drug-Free

Sometimes it seems that there is so much to do, and everything seems so urgent and important. This can feel overwhelming, and you can find yourself heading into a funk of feeling like "what's the use" and then be paralyzed into inaction. When these times set in, focus on the day at hand, dealing with things one task at a time. Just do what you can today and don't worry about tomorrow—until tomorrow. Take each day and each problem one at a time, doing the best you can with that single issue, and then move forward. As you make progress, you'll feel better about yourself, and your day will seem more manageable. On some days, especially when you find your coping skills at a low, handling the day and doing the best you can with that one day alone *is enough*. Be okay with it.

Taste-berry promise for the day: I will make a list of my tasks just for this one day at hand.

Forgiveness Is a Gift

When someone "lets you off the hook," it's a real gift.

Gregory Carl, 16
A Taste-Berry Teen's Guide to Managing the Stress and Pressures of Life

Have you ever messed up in a really big way and had someone "let you off the hook"? Didn't it feel like such a gift—and a huge relief? It is no accident that the center of the word "forgiveness" is the word, "give." We cannot demand forgiveness of ourselves or of others—it has to be given. It is a gift that recognizes that none of us are perfect; we are human and we make mistakes. This recognition that we are imperfect often lends the compassion and empathy to help us forgive others when they fall short and disappoint or hurt us. Forgiveness is always a gift, both to the recipient and the giver—for in forgiving others, we are better able to forgive ourselves. Practice forgiveness and watch how everybody benefits.

Taste-berry promise for the day: I will write myself a letter of forgiveness for a recent mistake I may have made.

We Are All Connected

I love people. A part of my self-worth will always be in relation to how I reach within myself and share myself with others.

Colleen Morey, 20
More Taste Berries for Teens

The Hawaiian Islands look like they're separate from each other, but they are not. While we see the mountaintops above the Pacific, there are deep valleys beneath the ocean that connect all the islands as one. This same connection exists for the human race. We may feel like we are separate from others, but actually we are all interdependent. You can get a sense of this oneness when you make a genuine effort to listen attentively to others; you can get it by being there to help them and to receive help from them. You know this sense of unity when you stop to acknowledge the blessing offered in a smile; when you make true eye contact and exchange kind words; or when you join with others in accomplishing some worthy goal. In these moments you know that we are all connected—and all one. This connection assures that in reaching out to help others, you also help yourself. Be a taste berry: Connect, assist and encourage others.

Taste-berry promise for the day: I will hug a friend and smile at the new person at school.

Respect Boundaries

*oundaries are about knowing what you want and
need, and standing your ground.*

Clark Brown, 15
Taste Berries for Teens #3

Do you have friends who act in a certain way when they're
around you, and act another way when they're with their other
friends—and who do this because you've let them know that
certain behaviors are acceptable to you, while others are not?
That's the way it works: Others almost always honor those values you find worth upholding. But, of course, they can only
honor what they know. This is why it's important to let others
know where you stand on things. Remember, others don't usually know what is and isn't okay with you unless you tell them.
Be willing to set boundaries—the sooner, the better. It's the taste-
berry thing to do: It's good for everyone. Standing your ground
serves as a guide for others—helping them offer the taste berry
of respect you desire.

Taste-berry promise for the day: I will make a list of
my five most important boundaries.

Be a Model of Peace

World peace starts with me living at peace with everyone in my life.

Hugh Benton, 17
More Taste Berries for Teens

Mahatma Gandhi's "be the change you want to see in the world" is more than sage advice. It is a blueprint for change—on a personal or global level. Consider its importance as it relates to world peace. As you live your life in peace with others—avoiding words and actions that spark animosity or anger, choosing kindness rather than criticism or violence—you model peace. Whether the change you'd like to see is in others or in your surroundings at school, at home or in your community, *being* that change is the first step in creating it. Consider it your taste berry to the world.

Taste-berry promise for the day: I will think of something I want to see changed in the way people treat each other at school and then practice "being that change."

Day
187

Listen Attentively

*E*ven if the other person has a completely different "take" on things—a totally different perspective than you do—that doesn't make that person wrong, or right, nor does it make your view better or second best.

Jon Branson, 16
A Taste-Berry Teen's Guide to Managing the Stress and Pressures of Life

You have one friend who believes both sexes should be allowed to play sports on the same sports teams and another friend who thinks it's a bad idea. Someone you know thinks prayer should be allowed in the schools, while another thinks it shouldn't. Is one set of ideas right, while the other is wrong? Maybe—but maybe not. And you won't know unless you hear both sides out. Allow others to express themselves fully—even when you may not agree with what they're saying. Attentive listening is the mark of an open-minded person. When you listen attentively, you show that you're comfortable with who you are and you don't have to make everyone else wrong so that you can be right. You've reached a point where you can say, "I don't see it that way, but I'd like to understand how you arrived at your view of things." Remember, being open to the views of others helps us gauge if our own view on things is on target—or not. Keep the view unobstructed—keep both your ears and your mind open.

Taste-berry promise for the day: I will practice hearing someone all the way through—with an open mind—and then respond by honestly sharing how I feel.

Have Fun with Friends

It's fun to hang out with a fun person who likes to have fun!

Marty LeBauer, 14
More Taste Berries for Teens

Doing things with someone you like and consider "fun" adds to the experience in just about every way. Even doing a "boring" homework assignment is fun if you're doing it with someone you like being with. Exchanging glances and laughter, sharing the new and old, big and small, and the awesome or awful, all remind you that you are connected, a part of something. The bonds of sharing sweeten life's joys, and ease the bitterness of its heartaches and losses. Union, having someone with whom to share your thoughts and experiences, being concerned with someone other than yourself, gives reason to life. Don't take the taste berries in your life for granted. Know who they are, honor them and be honorable: Do those things that keep these relationships full of life, full of meaning and full of fun.

Taste-berry promise for the day: I will call a friend to make plans for a great weekend day together.

Day
189

Eye-to-Eye with Your Parents

When my parents and I are seeing eye-to-eye, I find that I'm in a really "good space."

Megan Burres, 16
Taste Berries for Teens

Have you ever had an argument with your parents in the morning and the rest of the day everything was just off? Or have you ever had a sincere, loving, heart-to-heart talk with your parents and had it make your whole day seem better and brighter? Even though your days are busy with friends and school and life outside the home, your relationship with your parents is still very important to you and affects how you feel about yourself and life in general. Being on good terms with them is crucial to your sense of happiness and well-being. When all is well with your parents, it seems somehow easier to get through challenges and day-to-day life. Be a taste berry: Do your part to see eye-to-eye with your parents—do those things that keep your bonds with them strong and loving.

Taste-berry promise for the day: I will give my parents a hug and tell them how much I appreciate them.

Be Assertive

It's really important to be assertive—but without using intimidation or allowing yourself to be intimidated.

Jennifer Leigh Youngs
Taste Berries for Teens Journal

Have you ever wanted to say something, stand up for yourself or voice your view of things, but you just couldn't seem to get the words out? Did it simply seem easier to "let it go"? While there is a time and place for compromises, there is also a time and place for making certain that you are heard. Even when you are willing to compromise, you should be able to express your feelings and thoughts on a subject. Sometimes, this requires being assertive, which is part of being able to communicate in a positive, meaningful way. Good communication is important to building strong, respectful relationships. How do you practice this kind of communication? Speak clearly and confidently. Say what you mean and mean what you say. Do so in a courteous way so others will not be "turned off" or think you have an "attitude." Exercise the same respect you appreciate from others. Speak in a tone that conveys that you want to both understand and be understood. When you communicate in an honest, respectful and direct manner, everyone wins.

Taste-berry promise for the day: I will try starting my sentences with the words "I feel" when I'm talking about something that is emotionally charged.

See Others in a Positive Light

It is our obligation—as much as it is our honor—to help others see their lives in the most positive light.

Bettie B. Youngs
Taste Berries for Teens Journal

There are a lot of ways to help others see their lives in the most positive light: from encouraging them in the day, to supporting them in their dreams for the future. This obligation and honor present many opportunities for expression. As brothers and sisters in the human family, we are in some ways responsible and accountable to and for each other—thus we have an "obligation" to each other. The word "honor" means both privilege and freedom. When we help others see their lives in the most positive light, these pieces fall together. Freely acting on our belief that we are each accountable and responsible for each other, we experience the meaning and satisfaction that come from practicing this privilege. Be a taste berry who practices this loving privilege each day.

Taste-berry promise for the day: I will tell three people two things they say or do that are really positive.

191

Show Up for Life

*B*e smart—don't mess up; "show up" for your life.

Bettie B. Youngs
A Teen's Guide to Living Drug-Free

"Showing up for your life" means you are fully present—which requires being drug-free. As a result, you're better able to be a loving person and to feel the love that flows to you. You're better able to think about what you want in relation to who you are, and to uncover your talents, interests and aptitudes. You're better able to share your joy, express your concerns, and ask for help and support when you're facing tough times and trying situations. You're better able to feel that life is meaningful, and just as you need others, you can be of service and assistance to others. You're better able to decide what you want to achieve on a daily basis, as well as plan for your future. You're better able to handle the tough times without blowing them out of proportion, and to cope with your problems effectively. You're better able to be an inspiration and an encouragement to others. The rewards are simply "boundless" and excellent reasons not to use drugs and alcohol. The rewards are *life*—and living it at its fullest. Say "yes" to life. Say "yes" to living drug-free.

Taste-berry promise for the day: I will make a list of all the rewards I have in my life—and all those I'm looking forward to in the future.

Practice Confidence

A winning day is all about confidence, confidence, confidence!

Peggy Nunziata, 17
More Taste Berries for Teens

Have you ever wanted to win something—such as a spot on a sports team—but been so afraid you wouldn't make it that you didn't even try out? Almost everyone feels unsure of herself from time to time—no one knows for certain that all their goals and plans are "sure things." No one knows for certain that they will always win at everything they try or that everything is always going to go their way. If you wait around for absolute assurance, you won't move ahead in life. It can take confidence to go after your goals. The good news is that confidence can be developed through practice and experience. So set goals and make plans: Begin. Go forward. Doing this creates experience—much of which is sure to include success. As you begin to count your accomplishments, you'll find that you've developed confidence in yourself! Begin to build that confidence. Count all your winning days.

Taste-berry promise for the day: I will hang a calendar in my room and note each day I've accomplished progress on my goals with a star, a check or another symbol to remind me that I'm winning.

Love Yourself

Love demands that you save some of it for yourself.

Lisa Ritchey, 16
Taste Berries for Teens

Think of some of the ways you show love to those for whom you care deeply: You treat them with tenderness and care; you protect them in all the ways you can; you're kind, considerate, courteous and show appreciation for the things they do; you're careful with their possessions; you extend friendliness to those they care about. These are some of the many ways we demonstrate love. Showing love to others usually means we are loved in return—but not always. Even should those you love not love you in return, you still have someone who always loves you when you love yourself. You are your first and primary source of love. Consider it your obligation—as much as your honor—to love, respect and care for yourself. In a real sense, you are then never without love. Though you can give ample amounts away, you possess its source, a never-ending spring, and so you are never without it.

Taste-berry promise for the day: I will do something fun today that helps me celebrate how much I love myself.

Use Stress to Your Advantage

I like stress. I "eat it" for motivation.

Joshua Thomas, 15
A Taste-Berry Teen's Guide to Managing the Stress and Pressures of Life

Your body is doing its remarkable work when it lets you know that it "feels" stress. Quite simply, stress is our body's response to any stimulus—to the things going on around us, its goal being to alert us to the impending possibility that we may need to take action (such as run for cover!). While stress is your body's reaction, it's not your reaction. You get to decide how you will respond to the cues or the signals your body is sending. How do you respond? Do you get alarmed and fearful and therefore react with anxiety? Or do you use its energy to take action and get going? You get to decide. Learn all you can about how to use stress productively. You can keep your cool under pressure. Be a taste berry: Use stress to your advantage.

Taste-berry promise for the day: I will check out the Internet or go to the library to find a great new tip for dealing with stress.

Choose Your Attitude

I think grouchy old people were grouchy young people—and people who are full of life and fun when they are old were full of life and fun when they were young, too. My hope is to be forever young at heart.

Lerissa Dennison, 15
More Taste Berries for Teens

If you think about it, you probably know a lot of people of all different ages who are full of life and fun. Old, young or in between, you can be sure at some point this "life and fun" was their choice. When we accept our right and responsibility to choose our attitude, we can find great hope in believing the best is here and now, and there's even more to come. If today is great and we have the power to choose for tomorrow, too, then it's sure to be full of good things, as well. After all, with all that day-to-day experience, we're sure to become experts on how to create this good. Choose to be full of life and fun.

Taste-berry promise for the day: I'm going to be a playful person and dance around my room to my favorite music after school.

Seek Out Role Models

When someone is certain about what he or she stands for, it helps me "step up a notch" in terms of my expectations for myself.

Larry Epling, 19
More Taste Berries for Teens

Think of those of your friends who are most certain of what they stand for. Do they bring out the best in you? When you spend your time with people who act according to strong, positive values, it has a favorable effect on you: It raises your expectations of yourself. Perhaps this is partially because you have a role model who demonstrates "the way" to live with integrity. Maybe it is partially because it calls you to examine what it is you value and how it is you can live those values. Or perhaps it's because being around such people can make you feel so much better about the world in general, that it makes you feel better about yourself. That's the power of being with those who practice integrity: They are uplifting and motivating. Grow as a taste berry: Seek out these positive people and nurture your relationships with them.

Taste-berry promise for the day: I will thank those people in my world who model integrity—and tell them how much they inspire me.

Show Love by Your Actions

It's one thing to say "I love you," and another to show it. Actions speak as loud as words—and sometimes, louder.

Bettie B. Youngs
More Taste Berries for Teens

Have you ever known someone who just wasn't big on words, but whose every caring action demonstrated love? Or someone who spoke words of love, but treated you carelessly? Words, of course, have their place and their power, but actions are what bring those words to life. When you care about others, you treat them with respect; you respect the value they place on the people they love and on their possessions; you help them when they're in need; you are kind, encouraging, caring, appreciative. When it comes to love, the old adage, "Actions speak louder than words" definitely applies. Be a taste berry: Let your actions speak loud and clear of your love.

Taste-berry promise for the day: I will make certain that I'm home on time as one way to let my parents know that I love and respect them.

Day
199

Have Hope

Almost every great hope carries with it at least some degree of fear, since it's not yet a reality.

Jennifer Leigh Youngs
More Taste Berries for Teens

Our hopes move us forward in life: They give us a vision, a reason to strive, a goal to move toward. Having hope doesn't guarantee that we'll realize our vision, but it can help us be proactive in facing our fears. Without any hope we'd never move forward—the fear would leave us paralyzed. When a vision seems especially grand, it's easy for your hopes to raise to a place where you want it so badly that you feel the fear of its loss before it's ever even a reality—you're afraid to try to reach it, afraid of failure. Facing your fears, you gain the experience, confidence and strength of character you need to see your hopes become realities. Practice this courage.

Taste-berry promise for the day: I will journal on one of my fears and the first step I need to take to move through it.

Take Action

If you want to know who is going to be an achiever, look for the person with great focus.

Bettie B. Youngs
A Taste-Berry Teen's Guide to Setting & Achieving Goals

Have you ever wondered where to start on something—whether a project for school, getting a part-time job or accomplishing some other goal for yourself? You see the final destination and stare at it, trying to figure out what it'll take to get you from here to there. In the end, one thing is certain: "Getting there" requires action. Decide what you can do to get there and do it; then look at what you need to do next and do that. Start the journey to your destination one step at a time and keep on moving toward it. It sounds simple; let it be. The best solutions can usually be found in the simplest of actions: Achievers focus their time task by task by task until their mission is accomplished. Harvest taste berries of achievement; focus on the task at hand.

Taste-berry promise for the day: I will complete my homework as soon as I get home from school.

Send Love into the World

*T*here isn't a person in the world who doesn't want to
love someone.

Amanda Mossor, 17
More Taste Berries for Teens

Do you sometimes envision living in a world where love
works its magic everywhere and for everyone? If we *all* do our
part, we could bring to fruition this noble and impassioned
vision. We must each be willing to respect and care about our fellow travelers. When we love others, our actions resonate positive
feelings, sending these positive vibrations into the world.
Luckily, there is no shortage of ways to send love into the world.
Consider all those who we're given to love: parents, brothers and
sisters, grandparents, aunts, uncles, cousins, friends, a special
someone and pets—just to name a few. Be a taste berry: Send
love into the world and start by expressing it to those at home.

Taste-berry promise for the day: I will do an extra
household chore without mentioning it to anyone.

Celebrate Your Freedoms

Freedom — like life — is fragile.

Megan Mazzola, 18
Taste Berries for Teens #3

Have you ever stopped to think about all the freedoms we enjoy as Americans? Each weekday you wake up and head off to experience one of them: the freedom to receive an education. There's also your freedom of speech. The First Amendment of the U.S. Constitution gives every citizen the freedom to express his opinion about our government, culture or society. Elsewhere in the world, there are countries where people are jailed for speaking out on such subjects. We have the freedom of worship, the freedom to choose our religion, to practice our faith—or to forego any of these if we so choose. There are countries whose citizens are not allowed to practice their faith openly and would cherish having such freedom. Freedom means you are at liberty to choose what is best and meaningful for you; it means you have a voice and are allowed to use it. Treasure your taste-berry freedom and honor it: Exercise it wisely.

Taste-berry promise for the day: I will make a collage about what freedom means to me, and when my friends comment on it, I'll discuss how important it is that we all think deeply about the importance of freedom and how to ensure it.

Share Your Love

*B*eing in love can be a good thing—and not just for those who are in love. Their love makes the whole world a better place!

Janine Ito, 15
More Taste Berries for Teens

Love! Such a wonderful feeling! Feeling loved is likely to add a bounce in your step and help you feel kindly toward everyone you meet. Your homework is done, and it somehow didn't seem like such a drag—just another activity in your life—a life that has taken on more beauty since you've fallen in love. Suddenly, you seem filled with more goodwill, tolerance, patience and kindness. Your life has more meaning, and you want to share more of yourself with others. What a wonder this overflowing love can be: As it spills from your heart it can spread beauty to everyone in your world. Who is it that you love? Nurture and share your love today.

Taste-berry promise for the day: I will share a smile and a cheerful greeting to everyone I see today.

203

Create Synergy

The adage "1 + 1 = 3" is a real stress-buster!

Brenda Walters, 16
A Taste-Berry Teen's Guide to Managing the Stress and Pressures of Life

Do you have a zillion things to do and wonder how you'll ever get them all done on your own? Consider asking your "support team"—those who are there for you and stand by you through "thick and thin"—for help and support. The 1 + 1 = 3 adage implies that the "synergy"—the care and support—of even just one other person is so helpful that it feels as though the two of you are really three. This can help you feel supported and less alone as you face your schedule, your moments of "overwhelm" and when you're just tired and not really feeling up to your best. Don't be shy; you don't have to go it alone. And when you see someone else who is under a lot of pressure, don't forget to be a taste berry and offer your support.

Taste-berry promise for the day: I will determine who makes up the other half of my 1 + 1 equation.

Improve Your Community

We must love the community where we live. How we treat it shows how we really feel about our Earth home, about each other and about ourselves, as well.

Bettie B. Youngs
More Taste Berries for Teens

Is there someone in your town who rallies the community to do some awesome things, such as sponsoring a burn center for children, or a hospice, or championing programs for kids such as the Big Brothers Big Sisters program? Isn't there something very touching about these actions? Do they inspire you to think about how you can help others? True community is a kinship of caring: When people think about each other's needs, towns and cities are transformed into communities. Be a taste berry: Do your part to make your town or city such a community.

Taste-berry promise for the day: I will ask my parents how I might do something for our community.

Be an Optimist

Being an optimist is not an inherited trait; it's a learned response.

Jennifer Leigh Youngs
A Taste-Berry Teen's Guide to Managing the Stress and Pressures of Life

Do you have friends who automatically see the "up" side of things, while others always see the "down" side of things? Why do you think this is so? Do you think "seeing the cup as half-full" rather than "half-empty" is a genetic trait, and therefore some have it while others do not? Yes, that sounds ridiculous. In fact, being an optimistic person is not a biological gift, but a choice we make. Why focus on the negative when you can choose to see the positive? Not only does being an optimist make you more pleasant to be around, but it also helps you see the *possibilities* in life. Choosing to be as positive as you can be, to see things as bright as they can possibly be viewed, is also a taste berry for those around you: It helps them to do their best and strive for the best. Your optimism can make a lot of people happy!

Taste-berry promise for the day: I will start a gratitude list and remember to review and add to it each day.

"Act as If"

I "act as if" I belong, my goal being to convince myself that soon I will belong.

Desiree Huerta, 15
More Taste Berries for Teens

Have you gone to a social gathering and felt out of place, so you tried making the best of it, even acting as if you were having a nice time? If you're feeling like you don't belong, "act as if" you fit right in. If you're scared, "act as if" you're brave and at ease. If you're feeling out of sorts or sad, "act as if" you're happy. "Acting as if" is a great tool for facing and getting through many uncomfortable feelings. This isn't so you can fool yourself or anyone else into believing you feel differently. It's so you can *practice actually feeling differently.* As they say, "practice makes perfect." You'll find that although you started out "acting as if," you soon actually "feel as if."

Taste-berry promise for the day: I will practice being secure and confident by "acting as if."

Be a Positive Example

I think the goal is not just to be good and stay out of trouble in life, but to make your life a positive example for others.

Lennie Frazier, 14
More Taste Berries for Teens

Whose life serves as a positive example for you? What does this person do that inspires you and calls you to be better? How do you think you can live your life so that you help bring out the best in others? You never know the lives you touch by your example. Usually, it isn't a person's words or shining successes that make the biggest difference and help others most. What has the power to make the greatest difference and help others the most is the example of a life lived with integrity, one that is filled with daily acts of kindness, mostly small, yet meaningful in their purity and consistency. Make your life a positive example by being a taste berry each day.

Taste-berry promise for the day: I will help a classmate with an assignment he or she doesn't get but I understand.

Do Something Different

If you always do what you've always done, you'll always get what you've always got.

Adam Mason, 16
A Teen's Guide to Living Drug-Free

It takes a change in actions to achieve a change in results. For example: If you want to stop having arguments with your friends, you need to do something different. Perhaps you need to learn to be more patient and tolerant, to listen more attentively or to practice more tact and diplomacy when you share your opinions; or maybe you need to say how you feel sooner, before you get angry and blow up. The point is: It takes change of action to create change of outcome—and you are responsible for taking that action. So why do you sometimes continue to do the same things and expect different results? Although all of life is a series of changes, big and small, knowing this doesn't always take the fear out of change. You're familiar with what you know—and change brings the unknown: You don't know if you'll fail. You don't know "how" to do things differently—that is, until you do them! Overcome these fears: Do something different—take action and create the change you desire in your life.

Taste-berry promise for the day: I will try out for a team or pursue a dream I've always wanted to make real.

Be There for Others

Helping and comforting others is how we show our finest hour of being human.

Bettie B. Youngs
Taste Berries for Teens

Have you ever been there to help someone when they needed you—to give them a hug or a shoulder to cry on—and felt a fullness in your heart that struck at your deepest core? In these moments of giving to others, deep inside we know: "I was born to this." This knowledge is empowering. Those times when we are there to help others with a pure heart and a sincere desire to be of genuine support—no matter how trivial our gestures of support may sometimes appear—define our greatest purpose. You have the power to live this purpose. Be a taste berry: Help and comfort those who need it and experience your finest hour of being human.

Taste-berry promise for the day: I will ask a school counselor about becoming part of the peer-counseling program at our school—or ask how to get one started if there isn't one in place yet.

Everyone Is Unique

Always remember you are unique, just like everyone else.

La Rochefoucauld
A Teen's Guide to Living Drug-Free

There's no denying you are an original—no one else has your exact DNA, or identical thoughts, ideas and perspective on life. Wow! This can make you feel pretty special, and you *are* very special—just like everyone else! It is precisely because you have come to know and value yourself as special that you can come to appreciate that everyone in the world is also special. As such, everyone is entitled to the essentials in life—food, shelter, clothing—as well as a life free of oppression and filled with security and dignity. This is all the more reason why each and every one of us needs to fulfill our role in being a taste berry: Decide to be interested in civics and current events, take the time to read the newspaper, and engage in discussions about the conditions of the world and its citizens. Knowing what's going on for others on the planet prepares us for taking action to help when we are able. When we do this we show that we *understand* that others are special, too.

Taste-berry promise for the day: I will read the world news today and discuss with my parents why I feel everyone in the world is "equal," "special" and "deserving."

Accept Compliments Graciously

If you want to see how someone really feels about herself, pay her a compliment—and see how she treats it.

Jennifer Leigh Youngs
Taste Berries for Teens #3

Self-worth—what we think about ourselves—shows up in the things we say and do, even in the way we receive compliments. Have you ever noticed how many people squirm when they receive a compliment? Do you ever get uncomfortable when you receive one? You shouldn't. You see, a compliment is someone else's opinion, their positive appraisal. Don't step on that person's worthy evaluation. Ask yourself, "Who am I to negate this person's assessment of me?" So accept their comment graciously, thank them and allow their compliment to find a home in your heart. It's important to learn how to receive praise. How do you learn how to accept compliments graciously? When someone praises you, simply say, "Thank you," without giving in to any urge to minimize being worthy of the praise. Be a taste berry: Give your share of compliments each day—starting with the face in the mirror.

Taste-berry promise for the day: I will accept compliments graciously.

Learn from Your Embarrassment

If you've ever tripped right in plain view of someone you were trying to impress, you know you can survive anything!

Tony Johnson, 17
More Taste Berries for Teens

Do you know what it's like to want to impress someone and to have disaster strike? Your words come out all wrong, or you say something only a cartoon character could come up with or you unexpectedly burp? Have you ever been dumped by a friend, and everyone at school knew it? Everyone has gone through experiences when they felt totally mortified. Perhaps at the time you even felt as if you'd never get over your feelings of sheer embarrassment. Fortunately, human beings are remarkably resilient: We can get through even what seems like the most embarrassing of times. We not only "get over it," but having felt "it" firsthand, we learn the importance of compassion and empathy—which are some pretty impressive attributes to own. Put them into practice: Comfort or support others in their embarrassing moments; do all you can to make them feel less humiliated.

Taste-berry promise for the day: I will show empathy for those caught in embarrassing moments.

Find Your Voice

You've got to find your voice, and then speak it. How else do you define yourself? How else will anyone really know you?

Jennifer Leigh Youngs
Taste Berries for Teens Journal

You're hanging out with several friends, and one of them starts a conversation about smoking marijuana, saying that using "just a little" isn't all that big of a deal. You're positive that you don't want to use drugs, and that even "experimenting" is out of the question for you. What does finding your voice mean in this moment? When you find yourself in situations where it's hard to speak up, it is probably a good indication that it's time to do just that. Be true to yourself at all times. When you feel your conscience, instinct or intuition nudging you to use your voice, take the hint and speak up loud and clear. Be a taste berry to others, as well as to yourself: Make certain that you're heard. If it's not appropriate to say something, let your actions do the "talking."

Taste-berry promise for the day: I will set healthy boundaries and be clear on the choices I make.

Family Bonds

My very best friends are the members of my family.
Carrie Hague, 17
More Taste Berries for Teens

Have you ever walked into the house and had your mother or father (or brothers and sisters) take one look at you and know that you had a totally wonderful—or awful—day? As a family, do you ever reminisce or laugh together over some long ago family outing or event? The bonds of family are often the most powerful in our lives, profoundly affecting how we feel about ourselves; in turn, they contribute to how we cope with life. Hopefully, your family members are among your very closest friends—your #1 fans, always on your side, there with love and respect to support you and share your life—no matter what. Should you feel as if there are members of your family with whom you are less than "friendly," reach out and model the friend you'd like them to be—offering love and kindness, letting them know how important a strong and healthy family is to you.

Taste-berry promise for the day: When my mom or dad asks me how my day went, after answering the question, I'll ask about their day in return.

Be a Good Friend

All it takes is just one other person to make you feel as though you're not alone in the world.

Shire Feingold, 14
Taste Berries for Teens

Has someone ever reached out to you when you felt out of place, lost or lonely? It's amazing the effect just one person taking the time to connect and care can have. A friend who is there to listen can make the difference between hope and despair. When someone takes the time to smile and treat you with respect and interest, it can make you feel important. Imagine, just one person can make you feel that way! Just one person is all it takes to say, "I am not alone; I have a friend." Be a taste berry: Be that one person in someone else's life today.

Taste-berry promise for the day: I will invite a friend who is having a rough time to come over to my house for dinner.

Make Positive Decisions

My decision not to use drugs or alcohol is a way of making sure I don't ever mess up my life—or hurt anyone else's.

Carrie Sharritt, 16
A Teen's Guide to Living Drug-Free

The decision to remain drug- and alcohol-free is one of the best and most important ones you will ever make. It helps avoid so many painful experiences—from not being fully present in your own life, to possibly suffering the consequence of becoming chemically dependent. And, of course, using alcohol or drugs cannot only ruin your life, but potentially hurt others, as well. Making the choice to be drug-free is certainly a decision and an attitude you want to share with your friends. Most teens who end up with a drug or alcohol problem say that they got started because a friend turned them onto it. You have the power to counter this negative influence by serving as a positive example and influence to your family and friends. Surely such service is a taste berry with far-reaching effects. Look after yourself and others—be a positive influence in your world.

Taste-berry promise for the day: I will make a pact with a friend to always support each other in staying drug-free.

Love Has Many Lessons

essons on love provide an honors course in being a taste berry!

Trisha Gerald, 18
More Taste Berries for Teens

Have you ever loved someone, but that person "left" you? Or were you the one who left the relationship because it wasn't right for you? Did you then give up on love, or did you want to love yet again, and are you still hopeful that you will? The answer is simple, isn't it? There's no giving up on love. The heart wants to give love and be loved—time and time again. It just won't give up on love! Perhaps it naturally senses that it has so many more lessons on love yet to learn. That we want to be loved, and want to love others, speaks to the miraculous determination of the human heart to seek what it needs. With love—whether given, received, gained or lost—there always comes so many lessons. What have you learned about how to love yourself? What have you learned about how to better love others? Learn the lessons love teaches. They are among the most profound "studies" you will ever undertake!

Taste-berry promise for the day: I will think about the importance of being a loving person and write a song title for all the lessons love has taught me.

We All Make a Difference

If you feel unneeded, unwanted, like you can't possibly make a difference, then you need to know two things—one, you're wrong; and two, you need to "get a life!"

LaToya Jones, 17
Taste Berries for Teens

It's easy to convince yourself that there's really not that much you can do to help in any significant way. You may even believe that what you do won't make a difference—you're just one person. Yet each of us is important when it comes to making a difference in the lives of others. Each time we do our part to bring comfort to another person, we do our part to bring more love and light into the world. Helping just one person changes his or her life and experience of the world. One by one is how we can change the world. One day at a time, one person at a time, one by one by one. What one person, what one action, will you begin practicing this with today?

Taste-berry promise for the day: I will make a list of all the ways I might help change the world one person at a time.

Connect with Others

We're all here traveling through life together so we might as well talk with each other so we all feel less alone.

Tsinsue Chen, 16
More Taste Berries for Teens

What is your "policy" on chitchatting with others you meet? When you get in an elevator, do you stare blankly, watching the numbers go up and down, or do you strike up a conversation? Have you ever been in a long line at the store and started talking to someone next to you? Didn't you enjoy the momentary exchange, thinking the other person saw you as an open and approachable person? Moments of connection to other people can be bright spots in their day—and in yours. You never know what you might give or receive: comfort, perspective, humor, insight or just a welcome distraction from a problem. Even momentary exchanges—because they demonstrate a greater sense of belonging—can help you feel the worth of being human. Be a taste berry to fellow travelers you pass along the way as you journey through life.

Taste-berry promise for the day: I will chat with someone standing next to me in line at the store or in the cafeteria at school.

What Is a "Good" Family?

It's the way each person in a family makes concessions for each other that makes it a "good" family—or not.

Craig Buell, 16
A Taste-Berry Teen's Guide to Managing the Stress and Pressures of Life

All of us have times when we think we belong to the most wonderful family in the world, and other times when we think we couldn't possibly be related to one another! But probably what we never doubt is our desire to be from a "good"—a "healthy"—family. While families may share many similarities with other families, there is no other family exactly like yours in the world. Of course, the people—the members of your family— are each unique, but the dynamics your family creates are unique as well. So what makes a "good" family? Perhaps the most important and truly identifying characteristic of a "good" family is the love and support its members share. They "go the distance" to care for each other, to "be there" for each other, time and time again. They comfort each other through the tough times and cheer for each other in the good times. Share the taste berry of love and support at home; look for the ways your family is "good" to each other.

Taste-berry promise for the day: I will talk to my siblings or my parents about all the ways our family is loving and supportive.

Look for Miracles

Some experiences in life are so perfectly timed and well-placed that there is no way to shrug them off as chance or coincidence, times when even luck and fate are ruled out as possibilities.

Megan Haver, 16
More Taste Berries for Teens

Think back to those times when things in your life were "so perfectly timed and well-placed" that they couldn't possibly be coincidence, luck, chance or fate. Maybe a long-lost friend called you right at a moment you were in need of just the kind of encouragement only that friend could offer. Or perhaps you decided to give up your Saturday to volunteer at a senior center only to discover that the person you'd had a crush on for nearly a year had just started to volunteer there. Or your car unexplainably died when the light turned green and after turning the ignition back on, you looked up to see a car speeding through the red light in the other direction—and realized you narrowly missed being in an accident. Those wondrous, awe-inspiring events could be called miracles. But to recognize miracles one must be open to mystery. To embrace the miraculous, one must accept that there are realities beyond our comprehension, orchestrated by something greater than ourselves. These experiences and this open acceptance of them can fill your life with greater hope, comfort and meaning. Open to the wonder of miracles in your life.

Taste-berry promise for the day: I will be thankful for the "miracles" in my life.

Day 223

Overcome Obstacles

If an obstacle stands in the way of your meeting your goal, you've got to take it out—or it'll take out your goal!

Brad Rogers, 17
A Taste-Berry Teen's Guide to Setting & Achieving Goals

Have you ever been totally prepared for a big test—you've studied and you're ready for it? On the other hand, have you ever taken a big test for which you were totally unprepared? If so, you've learned that either way the results of your preparation are going to show up come grade time! The same necessity for "prep time" holds true with reaching your goals. The better prepared you are, the better your chance of success. So when you've set goals, take a look at them and ask yourself, "What can throw me off course, here? What could keep me from meeting my goal?" Asking this question means you can then go about finding a solution. This holds true whether you're planning for the obstacles that could arise in reaching the goals for your week or your day, for the months ahead, or for your long-term goals of the distant future. A well-laid course is your best defense against obstacles that might sabotage your goals. Take the time to plan this defense. When it comes to any obstacle, remember to protect yourself: "Take it out," before it "takes out" your goal!

Taste-berry promise for the day: I will look over my goals and check for obstacles that could slow me down. Then I'll find ways to overcome the obstacles.

Cool Enough to Cope

Cool or ghoul—it's your choice.

Jennifer Leigh Youngs
A Taste-Berry Teen's Guide to Managing the Stress and Pressures of Life

Some days, it can seem like there are a zillion things to be "stressed-out" over, but remember you get to decide if you're going to be stressed-out or not. One good way to not let stress turn your day upside down is to think positive. For example, rather than saying, "I'll never finish all this homework," change your thinking to, "I can do this! One answer at a time, I'll get this homework finished." Your thoughts can be redirected—you can change a negative thought into a positive one. When your thoughts start getting negative, visualize a stop sign and literally say, "Stop! I can get this under control. I've been stressed-out before, and the world didn't end. Nor did my being stressed help matters." Remind yourself to take it easy and take it slow. Tell yourself, "I'm cool. I can handle this." Then begin making your way one step at a time. You can do it: Tell yourself that you really are cool enough to cope.

Taste-berry promise for the day: I will look in the mirror and tell myself, "I am cool, and I won't let stress keep me from meeting my goals."

Win at the Game of Life

You have to "win at the game of life." The way you live your life—the example you set—determines if you're winning, or losing, that game.

Brian Slamon, 16
More Taste Berries for Teens

Who are your role models who serve as examples of "winning at the game of life"? Would Tiger Woods be such an example—because he is a true gentleman, as well as a good sportsman? Perhaps your role model and example is closer to home: an excellent teacher or a loving and attentive parent. How does someone "win at the game of life"? You win by living with kindness, by being honest and doing your part to make the world a better place. You win by taking care of yourself, by setting goals and moving toward them. You win by being who you are, sharing this with others and appreciating each person you encounter. You win by taking the time to appreciate all the good in your life and in the world—and then going on to create even more good. What are *you* doing to "win at the game of life"?

Taste-berry promise for the day: I will make some kind of "trophy" and present it to someone close to me who I feel "wins at the game of life."

Reach Out and Help

*C*onsider that the person you help in passing was put in your path for a reason.

Jennifer Leigh Youngs
Taste Berries for Teens #3

How many times have you watched someone struggle and felt a nagging in your heart to do something to help? Did you follow your heart? Or were you afraid to risk rejection? Maybe you told yourself that if the person wanted help they'd ask for it. Or maybe you figured someone else would come along and help. When you find yourself in this situation, remember: This person was put in your path and brought to your attention for a reason—*you* are the one who is called on to help. *You* are the one who is meant to receive the warm satisfaction. You are the one who is meant to be that person's taste berry. Don't walk around such opportunities in your path: Follow your heart, reach out and help.

Taste-berry promise for the day: I will follow my heart and help anyone in need today.

Express Your Love

C'mon, be honest: Even when you cringe or blush as you look back at some of the ridiculous things you've said or done in the name of love, you then do it all over again when you're in love once more!

Kristi Powers, 14
More Taste Berries for Teens

Have you ever written a letter or a poem that declared your eternal friendship and given it to your friend—and later wished you hadn't? Have you ever bared your heart and told someone you were in love with him or her and then regretted it? Sure, you might "cringe or blush" when you think about some of the "crazy things you've said or done in the name of love"—but still you can't deny the magic and the joy you found in expressing your love at the time! Feelings of love and friendship just long to be expressed.

Taste-berry promise for the day: I will think about all the ways I've "grown" from being loved and by being a loving person.

Putting Things in Perspective

*hings aren't always as do-or-die as they first appear.
Deciding the world won't end is a real breakthrough.*

Jennifer Leigh Youngs
Feeling Great, Looking Hot & Loving Yourself! Health, Fitness and Beauty for Teens

Have you found yourself in a situation that you felt you just couldn't face? Have you ever felt as if you would just have to move away and go to a new school if your special someone broke up with you? Maybe you thought such a move was in order when you lost the class election, or after everyone howled with laughter at you when you gave a stupid answer in class. Almost everyone has had times such as these. When you find yourself in the middle of such a situation—fretting, worrying, unable to let it go—it's a good idea to remind yourself of everything that is going right in your world. This can help you take that first step back, away from the problem so you can see it in its proper perspective: While real, it's not the end of world!

Taste-berry promise for the day: I will make a written inventory of all the good things in my life.

Pay Attention to Your Instincts

All the answers you'll ever need in life are within you. So listen to your instincts. And never sell out on your heart.

Bettie B. Youngs
More Taste Berries for Teens

Did you ever see someone and feel instant love, attraction and connection? Or have you ever been about to do something when a feeling fills you with the clear knowledge that "this isn't a good thing to do?" Oh, for the majesty of the heart! It is always there to guide you. Deep down inside, you know what is right and what is wrong. When you find yourself in a situation that feels uncomfortable or dangerous, you can feel it within your heart. When you find yourself being moved to comfort, share or give to someone, you just know it is right because you feel it in your heart. Don't ignore these instincts. Listen carefully, for within your heart lie taste berries of love and wisdom—from which so many important answers flow.

Taste-berry promise for the day: I will journal about all the messages my heart has shared with me today.

Face Your Fears Head-On

acing your fears head-on increases the chances of having your hopes realized.

Jennifer Leigh Youngs
A Taste-Berry Teen's Guide to Managing the Stress and Pressures of Life

If you tiptoe around your fears, wait for them to melt away all on their own, or deny their existence and avoid them all together, you lose the chance to conquer them. If those fears happen to stand in the way of your goals, you can also lose or delay the opportunity of realizing your dreams. It takes courage to march bravely through your fears. But know that bravery doesn't exist without the fear that requires it to be put into action. Fear is a normal part of life—a natural by-product of going forward, making changes and experiencing new things in life. When you confront your fears in spite of the temptation to avoid them, they become a part of your past that much more quickly. So keep your sights on the goal of having your hopes realized and move forward through your fears. What is the taste berry of hope on the other side of the biggest fear you are facing?

Taste-berry promise for the day: I will talk to my best friend about any fears I have when it comes to my goals.

Choose Your Friends Carefully

*S*eek *friends who are positive and optimistic people, those who bring out the best in you: It'll make you a better, and happier, person.*

Bettie B. Youngs
Taste Berries for Teens #3

An optimistic friend uplifts you and shows you how to be grateful for all the good in your life. It is in this sort of relationship that you view life from a positive angle. This can be a big help. Seeing the cup half-full as opposed to half-empty is good for your physical and emotional health, and helps you do and be better. Take this into account when you're seeking out friends. Keep in mind that those who are positive and optimistic can have a really positive and optimistic influence on your life. Choose those kinds of friends—and be one to others.

Taste-berry promise for the day: I will tell my friend two good reasons why I am grateful for our friendship.

Don't Suffer Alone

Some challenges are simply too big for anyone to handle alone.

Samil Ousely, 15
More Taste Berries for Teens

If you are sick, you see a doctor. If your car is broken, you see a mechanic. If you need help understanding an assignment, you ask the teacher about it. These challenges and many others are best solved with help. We all need help with any number of obstacles along life's path, whether it is overcoming heartaches, grief or other circumstances too big to cope with on our own. Sometimes it's difficult to let others know that you need help; you may be ashamed, embarrassed or feel vulnerable. You may even think that you're supposed to deal with challenges on your own. Or you may be tempted to run from them or pretend they don't exist. Rather than act on these urges, reach out for the help of others. This is a sign of wisdom and maturity. Not only can it lend you the comfort and strength to get to the other side of your problems, but it also allows others to nourish their hearts as they connect with you in compassionate and caring ways. If you are facing struggles that seem overwhelming, don't suffer alone; confide in those you trust.

Taste-berry promise for the day: I'll think of two people who most help me make it through difficult times, and let them know how much I appreciate their love and support.

Nurture Your Faith

Faith ties us to the timeless truths of all humanity.

Bettie B. Youngs
More Taste Berries for Teens

When you believe in something greater, when you trust there is an essence that genuinely loves and cares in infinite ways, you tap into the source of miracles and wonders that are as old as time. As you take the time to deepen this belief and to exercise this trust, you will find comfort and energy that allow you to be more than you've ever been without them. Tap into this source by nurturing your faith.

Taste-berry promise for the day: I will take time to pray today.

Be Peaceful

*I*f you want to find yourself, look within.

Jennifer Leigh Youngs
Feeling Great, Looking Hot & Loving Yourself! Health, Fitness and Beauty for Teens

Take the time to be peaceful so as to listen to the voice within that guides and directs you. Allow this voice to remind you of what's right and wrong for you, and remind you of all the ways you are a good person. Allow this voice to bring you to a greater awareness of who you are and what you genuinely value. Receive the gifts this voice within has to offer: more love for yourself and others; the ability to see more of your own good and the good in the world; and greater peace, strength and courage.

Taste-berry promise for the day: I will take time to be alone and listen to my "inner voice."

See the Best in Others

I've come to the conclusion that jumping to conclusions is a total waste of time.

right
Tom Pierson, 16
Taste Berries for Teens

Have you ever thought someone didn't like you because she never spoke to you, and later found out she was just shy? Did you hear the new student at school had been kept back a year, and assumed he or she wasn't a good student—then found out that this person had been very ill and had to miss school? Have your friends ever stopped talking when you walked into the room, and you thought that they were talking behind your back—only to discover later that they'd been planning a surprise party for you? It's so important not to jump to conclusions or make assumptions. Feelings could get hurt—including your own. And, of course, there's the very real possibility your assumptions aren't anywhere close to what is really going on. The "taste-berry" conclusion is always one that sees the best in others—and also waits for all the facts.

Taste-berry promise for the day: I will see the best in myself and others.

center
235

Encourage Others to Soar

Encouragement is akin to growing wings so as to fly.

Jennifer Leigh Youngs
More Taste Berries for Teens

Has there been someone in your life who always encouraged you? Someone who absolutely believed you were awesome and capable of great things? Wasn't this person's presence in your life just "the best"? When someone loves and believes in you and your highest and best potential, that person gives you a source of hope, strength and courage, and empowers you as it feeds your own faith in yourself. When we have people like this in our lives, we are inspired to do and be our best. Elect to be such a taste berry in the lives of others: Believing in their best, encourage them to soar. In the process, you, too, will soar to greater heights!

Taste-berry promise for the day: I will tell a friend all the reasons I believe in him or her.

Be a Good Listener

Listening attentively can diffuse hurt, even anger.

Jennifer Leigh Youngs
Taste Berries for Teens #3

Disagreements don't necessarily mean a relationship is unhealthy or in trouble. Most close relationships—whether with friends, family or a special someone—have at least an occasional argument. The goal is to communicate in a way so as not to harm the relationship. When you listen attentively and talk in a loving, caring way, it can create a win-win proposition: Doing this, you win out over being at odds; you stay close, and even draw closer. Both people triumph! Always seek to offer others the taste berry of a heart and mind that is willing to listen—and you'll find yourself enjoying the taste berry of understanding.

Taste-berry promise for the day: I will practice being a good listener.

Be a Wise Judge

I grew up hearing, "Don't judge a book by its cover." To that I would add: Take the time to study its pages, so that you can judge accurately.

Jennifer Leigh Youngs
Feeling Great, Looking Hot & Loving Yourself! Health, Beauty and Fitness for Teens

Usually the old adage "don't judge a book by its cover" is used to remind us not to judge a person until we know him well enough to make a fair assessment. Perhaps the more important aspect of this message is that it asks us to gain a better understanding before making any judgment. There can be many things to consider beneath almost any surface. Gazing at the ocean, for example, you may think it appears peaceful and serene, while below its glossy surface it's teeming with a lively undersea world. "Don't judge a book by its cover" can have even greater implications: It can mean don't take the beauty of our planet for granted, nor the well-being of its people. Know what is going on globally, beneath the glossy surface of day-to-day life. Understanding is the key to judging accurately. Be a taste berry and learn all that can help you be of service to others, to the planet and to yourself.

Taste-berry promise for the day: I will read an article on the Internet or in the newspaper about the environment.

Have a Dream Machine

Everyone needs a "dream machine."

Bettie B. Youngs
A Taste-Berry Teen's Guide to Setting & Achieving Goals

You'll need a "dream machine" to reach your goals. What's a dream machine? A dream machine is the "mechanism" you use to think about all you want out of life. You need to be able to dream to create goals for your life. How do you learn to dream? One way is to hang around with interesting and creative friends who have big plans for their lives because being with them can stimulate you to "think big." And, you can read broadly, exposing yourself to great minds, which can expand your own sense of things. You can attend classes and seminars to stimulate your thinking, or you could watch TV shows and films that are interesting and educational. Of course, these are not the only ways to "think big," but the point is, you need to be able to dream and then set goals to make your dreams come true. Do all you can to rev up your dream machine and dream big—big enough to be your best in life!

Taste-berry promise for the day: I will watch an educational show or film and think about how it applies to the aspirations I have for my life.

Day 240

Find Humor in Life

**aughter is probably one of the best ideas God came up with.**

Martin Michaels, 14
More Taste Berries for Teens

Think back to a time when you and someone you love—whether a friend or family member—were laughing hysterically over something together. Or, recall the time you walked into a room and your friends were sharing a conversation that obviously was bringing great fun and joy to their time together. Didn't it feel great? Wasn't there a true connection in that shared laughter? Doesn't the happiness and connection live on as a truly special memory that adds to your relationship? The joy to be found in laughter celebrates life right here and now. When you choose and share laughter, you are choosing joy and connection. Being able to find the humor in a situation is a gift—and a blessing. It's also a skill that you can develop. It may take a little practice, but you can learn to see the gift and the joy in any situation. Practice finding the taste berry of humor where you once saw none.

**Taste-berry promise for the day:** I will share the humor in a situation with my friends today.

Have a Clear Conscience

When you do the right things, for the right reasons, the best things happen.

Bettie B. Youngs
A Teen's Guide to Living Drug-Free

There are times when it's fairly easy to "get over" on someone, to tell a little "fib," thinking no one will ever know the difference. But is that true? Will no one find out? The expression, "There is no pillow as soft as a clear conscience," implies that being "right with the world" is a good feeling. Certainly doing "right for the right reasons" benefits others. But your highest and best decision is *always* right for you. You've applied the test of truth and so you know that whatever happens as a result is okay. When you do the right thing, the outcome is always one you can live with. And you'll also sleep comfortably as a result. Always choose the "soft pillow" of a clear conscience.

Taste-berry promise for the day: I will be totally honest in all I say and do.

Be of Service

If you're open to helping others, usually you'll find the opportunity to do so right at the tip of your nose.

Randy Bobrow, 16
Taste Berries for Teens

Do you sometimes hear, "I'd like to get involved, but I don't know how"? Getting involved—helping others—is as simple as looking around right where you are. "Helping" doesn't have to only mean assisting on a "mega-scale"—such as going off to another country on a mission to build homes for those in need of safe shelter. Often, the most relevant place for you to make a difference is right where you are. Look to your own neighborhood, school or community: What is needed to make each place—and the people within—peaceful, safe and comfortable? Whether you decide to help an elderly neighbor with yard work, become a "peer counselor" at your school or join a neighborhood beautification project, opportunities to be of service abound. Do as much as you can for as many as you can—right where you are.

Taste-berry promise for the day: I will go through my clothes and donate those I don't need to a charitable organization in my community.

Day 243

$\mathcal{H}$ave a "$\mathcal{H}$eart-to-$\mathcal{H}$eart"

$\mathcal{Y}$ou've got to talk about what's important to you. Clarifying your aspirations is the first step in turning desire into a concrete plan of action.

Jeff Daniels, 17
More Taste Berries for Teens

Have you ever noticed how motivated and inspired you feel after talking about your hopes and aspirations with your parents or best friend? And don't you feel calmed and reassured after having a heart-to-heart about things that are bothering you? Discussing things with others helps you to "hear" yourself, and so you are able to clarify your real feelings about things. Talking with others also creates a level of accountability so you'll feel inspired to commit to doing what you profess to be of importance. Sharing with others is how we really learn what we're thinking and feeling. It's also how we gain the support of others in going forward. Who are those taste berries in your life that make it safe for you to talk over anything that's on your mind and in your heart? Talk with them. And don't forget to thank them for being taste berries in your life.

Taste-berry promise for the day: I will talk over what I want to do and be in life—my aspirations—with a good friend.

Look Through Divine Eyes

*W*hen I had something on my mind, talking it over with my grandmother was especially gratifying because she saw life through divine eyes, and so the answer was always a simple one.

Jennifer Leigh Youngs
Taste Berries for Teens #3

Do you know someone who always sees right through any problem, always finding a simple, yet "right-on" answer? Those who have a truly spiritual outlook—who see life through "divine eyes"—can be such a blessing. These loving and nurturing people have a way of making uncomfortable feelings and problems seem less overwhelming by presenting an eternal perspective. The love that is the essence of their faith can empower and strengthen, comfort and inspire. Who do you turn to when you're seeking the simple answers that can be seen through "divine eyes"? Take the time to let these taste berries know how they sweeten your life. And don't forget to be a taste berry who lets others see their lives through your own divine eyes.

Taste-berry promise for the day: I will journal about what it means to me to see life through divine eyes.

Release Your Pain

The more we try to hide our pain, the larger it gets, so it's as though we shine a spotlight on our suffering.

Jennifer Leigh Youngs
Taste Berries for Teens #3

Do you remember ever having a broken heart or being troubled? How was your pain brought to light? Hurting is a bell, a siren, reminding you how fragile you can be. Your ego may tell you to ignore it, or to hide it and not to let anyone know that you're vulnerable. After all, you are a bold and confident teen: You can hang tough. But hiding your pain is only holding on to it. Pain that is not released coils around your heart, binding you to your suffering. And so the suffering lingers. But when you shine the light of honesty and openness on your pain by admitting it exists—which is what you do by sharing it with someone—then the pain eases. Don't allow your pain to suffocate your heart. If you are holding on to a pain, confide in someone you trust and free your heart to heal.

Taste-berry promise for the day: I will go to someone I can trust and talk honestly about any pain I'm feeling.

Take Your "Vitamins"

Always be sure your daily diet is rich in sources of inspiration.

Jennifer Leigh Youngs
A Taste-Berry Teen's Guide to Setting & Achieving Goals

Can you think of someone who is always willing to tell you how cool, good, bold and wonderful you are? Is there someone who never fails to come up with some sort of praise for your latest success? Doesn't it make you want to get right out there and keep on going forward? Inspiration is like that. It's one of the best "vitamins" you can take! The good news is that you can be your own source of inspiration. Begin by being optimistic and hopeful. Your hopes inspire and motivate you, as they move you forward in life by giving you a vision, a reason to try, a goal to move toward. This gives you the attitude you need to make your hopes and dreams realities, as it helps you believe in yourself and go for it! You can then coach yourself and cheer yourself on. Look in the mirror, give yourself pep talks, and "Hey, you did it! Good for you!" messages. Be a source of your own inspiration!

Taste-berry promise for the day: I will inspire and motivate myself by looking in the mirror and giving myself a pep talk.

Be Healthy and Beautiful

*O*ffer up your brand of beauty; you are who the world
is waiting to see and learn about.

Bettie B. Youngs
Feeling Great, Looking Hot & Loving Yourself! Health, Beauty and Fitness for Teens

You carry your beauty with you every minute of every day,
every place you go. One of the great secrets of beauty is that it
comes from within. So your beauty is about who you are.
Nurture it: Value yourself—this means valuing your health.
Believe in yourself—this means being friends with the face in the
mirror. Have the courage to be an individual; be aware of those
around you, but don't forget that you are you. Appreciate yourself; learn to enjoy the feeling of being healthy and attractive on
your terms. Decide what healthy means for you—and be as
beautiful as you can be.

Taste-berry promise for the day: I will do something
special for myself to show I value and appreciate being who I
am.

Be Comfortable with Yourself

When a person is genuinely comfortable with who he is, it shows.

Jennifer Jones, 16
Taste Berries for Teens

There is something very "real" about the way people act when they are comfortable with themselves. There is a confidence that isn't cocky or overdone. Even when they get rattled or stressed-out, they seem to be able to admit it and handle it with a certain grace. You live with yourself day in and day out, no matter where you go or who else does or doesn't go along, so learning to be comfortable with yourself should be a priority. How do you learn to be comfortable with yourself? You learn this by being honest with yourself and others—in a word, "authentic." You act according to your values—this builds your self-esteem. You are considerate and kind—this strengthens your connection to others and to your own heart. You acknowledge your own successes—this increases your self-worth. And you learn from your losses—this gives you perspective and growth. Do these things knowing that you can be comfortable with who you are, and the whole world will know it.

Taste-berry promise for the day: I will have a discussion with my friends about how we can be more authentic with each other.

Friends Ease Stress

riends are a real plus when it comes to getting through a stressful day!

Kimmy Shavers, 14
A Taste-Berry Teen's Guide to Managing the Stress and Pressures of Life

How do your friends help you when you're in the midst of a stress-filled day? Do they help you work things through—perhaps just by being a listening ear? Maybe they also give you sound advice. Possibly your friends even get in there and take action—helping you study or lending you the perfect sweater to wear on the date you're stressing over. It may even be the fact that they accept you stress and all—all the time—that helps you get through your stressed-filled day. Sometimes you think that letting others see that you're having a tough time coping can make you look needy or nerdy. It can really help to have friends who you are certain will love and accept you even if you do look that way! Good friends are true assets. Let yours know how much you appreciate them. And don't forget to "be there" for your friends when you can see they are on overload!

Taste-berry promise for the day: I'll let my friends know I appreciate how they help me make it through stressful times.

Choose Happiness

eing kind shows that you are a happy person who likes herself.

Jennifer Leigh Youngs
Taste Berries for Teens

When you feel your happiest, doesn't it make you feel more kindly toward others? Generally, happy people are open to getting to know others better, so they tend to reach out and share their warmth. When you're genuinely happy with life and with yourself, being considerate and thoughtful is a natural response. The good news is that the choice to be happy is your own. Who wouldn't want to choose happiness? It feels good inside and reflects outside, making others feel good, too. It helps you to be kind to others and truly like yourself. It makes it easier to see the good in life and those who live in it with you. Choose happiness: The taste-berry rewards are obvious and sweet.

Taste-berry promise for the day: I will tell someone what is beautiful about today.

Use Your Coping Skills

There are always going to be tough times; there's simply no escaping them. But if you don't choose positive ways to cope, you can count on even tougher times ahead!

Paige Williams, 17
More Taste Berries for Teens

When your world seems to be falling in on you, it's no time to run—or hide! It's time to put your best foot—and skills—forward and find solutions. Stressful times can be disorienting, so it's especially important to be conscious of the decisions you're making. It's also an important time to take care of yourself, making sure you're getting the nutrition, rest and exercise you need to be your best so that you can face and get through a difficult situation. Make certain your support team is in place, and listen to their suggestions for getting the help and support you need. Take care of yourself, and make certain you are doing all the things you can to cope in positive ways. Just as you are compassionate with others when they're going through tough times, "be there" for yourself, as well.

Taste-berry promise for the day: I will make the effort to "check in" with the people I consider to be my support team.

You, Too, Can Be a Hero!

Heroes are made, not born. Decide to be a hero!

Bettie B. Youngs
Taste Berries for Teens Journal

Do you know a hero? Are you a hero? When you think about a "hero," does the image of courageous men and women who put their lives at risk to keep us safe come to mind? Or, do you think of someone who is braving a difficult challenge—such as actor Michael J. Fox, who is battling Parkinson's disease? Indeed, all these people are heroes. But sometimes daily living can be an act of courage, such as when you decide to act with integrity or persevere, no matter what. When you make this decision—to do what's right, to keep on going even when things are tough, to face your fears whatever they may be—you are deciding to be a hero, too. Be a hero: Practice courage each day in all that you do.

Taste-berry promise for the day: I will think about who my heroes are and what qualities they have that I want as my own.

Commit to Change

What I've learned about change is that the moment you commit, then angels guide.

Jenny Bilicki, 19
More Taste Berries for Teens

Have you ever committed to achieving something and felt as if there was something greater urging you on? Something beyond just your own desires and ambition? Often when you commit yourself to doing what it takes to make some change for the better in your life, it's as if everything in the entire universe unites to cheer you on, lighting your path to help you reach your goal. Everything unfolds in such a way that it seems as if more than just you wanted to see this change occur. What change for the better are you willing to sincerely commit to in your life? What greater good would you like to accomplish? Commit to this change today and watch for those special ways you can see "angels guide" as you make this change a reality.

Taste-berry promise for the day: I will take the first step in creating a change for the good in my life.

Do Good Deeds

When you share yourself in selfless ways, you teach a richer meaning of being a fellow traveler on the journey of life.

Becky Coldwell, 15
Taste Berries for Teens

Sometimes we may feel like we're only a single voice, one person, so how much can that really matter to the whole world? The much-admired Mother Teresa was fond of saying, "You make a difference in the world one, by one, by one." Believe that you do make a difference. We could all make the world a better place to live in if we each did our share of kind deeds. How can you personally make the world a better place? Carry out your share of good deeds each day. In the least, it will make the world a better place inside of you.

Taste-berry promise for the day: I will make a point to do two kind deeds today.

Trust in the Good

*T*he God I know is a kind and loving God, always looking out for His children—always arranging perfect ways to help them.

Megan Haver, 16
More Taste Berries for Teens

You've probably heard the saying, "When one door closes, another opens." Have you ever experienced it? Have you applied for a job you really wanted but didn't get, and then landed a job that you describe as "perfect for me"? Has the person you had a crush on gotten serious about someone else, and then a special someone far more suitable came along? Things don't always look the way we expect them to, even when they are unfolding perfectly. That's why we can find great comfort in trusting that when we do our best and then trust in a power greater than ourselves to do the rest, then what is best for us will happen. The outcome may not be when or what we expect, but we can trust that it will be exactly what it's supposed to be. Trust in the good and watch it unfold.

Taste-berry promise for the day: I will journal about those times when something "more perfect" than I had wanted happened for me.

Families Come in All Shapes and Sizes

M aybe someday we will erase the idea of families as "perfect" and look at them in a whole new light— like a place where each member helps the other deal with real issues in real life.

Craig Buell, 16
A Taste-Berry Teen's Guide to Managing the Stress and Pressures of Life

Television programs and preconceived ideas can send distinct messages about what a family is supposed to look like. When your family fails to fit this image, you may feel cheated out of the "ideal." The truth is that families are as varied as the people who make them up—even more so, since it's a group of people with a whole array of different personalities, creating family dynamics that are unique. Putting aside the myth of "perfection," regardless of the "size and shape" of your family, do your best to have loving relationships with each person in it. Try to help each one deal with real life and the issues that are a part of your family life. Appreciate what's good, and practice speaking and listening to your family members in ways that show you care. Your work as a taste berry is always in great demand—most especially at home with your family.

Taste-berry promise for the day: I will plan a special family time—such as popcorn and a video, or a pizza dinner—to celebrate what a "good" family we are and express my appreciation for them.

Choose Wisely

isdom is applying the best decision you can make at the moment.

Natasha Vesna, 15
More Taste Berries for Teens

How would you define wisdom? Does it seem like a lofty word or virtue—one you can't really own? Wisdom isn't nearly as unattainable as you might believe. Yet it *can* take strength to act on. It's thinking about what is the best thing for you to do and then doing it. Sometimes it can be tough to choose the best and right decision—no matter what. It may not always be the most popular choice and maybe, in making this decision, you won't be popular with those around you. But once you've weighed all the alternatives and you know this is what you have to do, continuing to choose wisely means you've done your best.

Taste-berry promise for the day: I will write my definition of wisdom and how I acted wisely today.

Memories Are Precious
Ties to the Past

A memory can be as powerful as the moment it happened.

Jennifer Leigh Youngs
More Taste Berries for Teens

Have you ever had a close friend who moved far away? What was the best time you ever had with this friend? Can you remember your first love? What was it that made you fall in love with this person? Perhaps you've lost a family member whose love will always live in your heart. You need only bring to mind your most cherished memories of loved ones to realize how valuable they are—recreating the moments, the love, the sense of connection. Memories are such precious ties to the past and to those times and those people whom we have loved—especially when they are no longer in our lives. It can be frightening to think we might forget and somehow lose those ties forever. Take comfort in believing that such memories cannot be taken from you. Even though you may think they are being buried in a blizzard of new memories and experiences, they will return to you again and again, just when you need them the most. Treasure these taste-berry memories and allow them to help sweeten the bitterness of loss and grief.

Taste-berry promise for the day: I will cherish my loving memories by writing a note to an old friend who has moved far away.

Be a Star!

You've got to look out for your self-esteem. It's your responsibility.

Jennifer Leigh Youngs
Feeling Great, Looking Hot & Loving Yourself! Health, Fitness and Beauty for Teens

How do you look out for your self-esteem? One good way is to have goals. What does setting and achieving goals have to do with your self-esteem? You know firsthand what you do, how you do it, and whether or not you are deserving. When you set goals, you see yourself as motivated. When you achieve goals, you see yourself as a capable and competent person. You have decided to accomplish something, worked hard to achieve it and met your agenda. You know you are worthy, and your self-esteem shoots skyward. You're a star, and you know it. And you've earned the right to shine as one. Feast on the taste berry of self-esteem—as you shine—and go on to reach for new and brighter goals.

Taste-berry promise for the day: I will talk about self-esteem with my friends and share ideas on how we can be supportive in looking out for each other's self-esteem.

259

Be "Rich" in Friends

Each new person represents a new possibility to see ourselves and our lives in a whole new way.

Anaïs Nin
More Taste Berries for Teens

Do you have one friend who always seems to make you laugh, and another who is a wealth of practical and wise advice? Is there one friend who can always tell you exactly what to wear to look your best, and another who knows the right thing to say when you're feeling down? While we all share similarities, no two of us are exactly alike. Each of us has learned our own lessons in life; each of us is viewing the world from the heart and eyes of our own being, with our own perspective. Each and every one of us has so much to share with one another. What one friend can share—an attitude, idea or perspective—will be his or her own, delivered in that person's own special way. This is why it is "rich" to have many friends. Stay open to the new possibilities that having an array of friends can bring.

Taste-berry promise for the day: I will introduce myself to someone I don't know at school.

Your Mistakes Can Help Others

Be the sort of person who wants to make a difference in someone's life.

Jennifer Leigh Youngs
A Teen's Guide to Living Drug-Free

Have you ever taught someone about a sport you've had your share of spills learning to master? Perhaps you've coached someone on how to avoid failing a driver's test you didn't pass the first time around. Maybe you've shared tips on how you survived a broken heart or losing a job. Perhaps your lessons came at an even higher cost, and you've shared the dangers of drinking or trying drugs. It can be a comfort to know that your painful experiences and mistakes are able to help someone else. You're likely to share your "hard-learned" lessons with a passion and conviction that rings true. Sometimes the lessons learned by someone who "screwed up" can have the greatest impact on someone headed in the same direction. A sort of amends can be made in this type of sharing. Great healing can be found in allowing your pain to be someone else's blessing. And great rewards are gained by such humility.

Taste-berry promise for the day: I will help someone else by telling them about a lesson I learned the hard way.

Cherish the Beauty and Power of Life

are about people . . . and always respect Mother Earth.

Bettie B. Youngs
More Taste Berries for Teens

Today, breathe in the air, gaze up at the sky and take notice of the life that teems around you: trees stretching and waving in the wind, flowers bursting with bright colors, countless blades of grass, butterflies fluttering from place to place, beetles and bees buzzing about, parading ants marching in rows throughout the flower beds and grass. It's awesome and wondrous—this abundance of life. Take a precious moment to acknowledge it. Connecting, appreciating and respecting life in all its forms helps you live with deeper satisfaction and meaning. As basic as these instructions seem, they ground you in an awareness of being part of something much bigger than yourself, as they feed your heart, your soul and your spirit. Life is filled with beauty and power; take the time and thought to recognize this. And make sure you do your part to protect it.

Taste-berry promise for the day: I will watch the sunset this evening.

Help Others Feel Less Alone

All of us—no matter how old or young—need others to show an interest, and to be patient and tolerant.

Carrie Hague, 15
Taste Berries for Teens

Everyone needs to know that others care. A small kindness, a bit of attention, a friendly ear or a warm smile—all can make a difference to someone else. It's surprising how little it takes to show that you care. Being there to help a friend in need can help your friend feel as if she really matters. Listening to an elderly person who you hardly know can help him or her feel regarded as the wise sage the years have created. Smiling or saying hello to another teen you pass in the hallway can help that person feel less alone. Being patient and understanding when the child you are baby-sitting is crying for her mother makes her feel more safe and secure. It can take so little to make a difference to someone else, to help another person feel less alone in the world. Be a taste berry: Care about all people and let them know it.

Taste-berry promise for the day: I will reach out to someone who looks lonely by smiling and asking about his or her day.

Love Is Unlimited

*W*ithout love in my life, I'd cease to exist!

Peter Colucci, 15
More Taste Berries for Teens

Are you "in love"—or hoping to be? Do you feel that without love, life would cease to have any meaning at all? Most people agree that love and love's meaning make the world go around! When deeply in love, looking for love or suffering heartache from love's loss, you may sometimes forget all the different ways that love can appear and take form in your world. Don't limit love—think of all the ways that it shows up in your life: your family, friends, a special someone, your pet—even in your passions in life. Every bit as important is your love for yourself. This is an anchor for all the other love in your life. In short, you can't love others if you don't love yourself.

Taste-berry promise for the day: I will listen to my favorite song about love and consider all the ways love shows up in my life.

Learn from Failure

Most successful people can tell you of times they did not succeed, and in fact, failed miserably. And each will tell you how important their failures were in eventually becoming a success.

Bettie B. Youngs
Taste Berries for Teens

Don't ever let a failure stop you from getting up and moving forward toward success. What sets successful people apart from "quitters" is their willingness to use "failure" as important information. Edison gave words to this perspective after he had failed to invent the lightbulb after a thousand tries—and was therefore called a failure by one of his colleagues: "No, I have not failed," Mr. Edison countered, "I have discovered a thousand ways it will not work!" So when you bomb out on something, try to nail down the reason. For example, should you get a lower score on a test than you'd like, you might honestly say, "Okay, my not studying (or getting enough sleep, or eating a power breakfast—you fill in the blank!) didn't work for me. Next time, I'd better . . ." Use all the facts—what works and what doesn't work—as important information to move you toward your goals. Then get up and get going—success is waiting for you!

Taste-berry promise for the day: I will learn from my failures and keep moving toward success.

Make Your Joys Your Job

eing happy in your "life-work" is about making sure you're doing what you should be doing.

Jennifer Leigh Youngs
A Taste-Berry Teen's Guide to Setting & Achieving Goals

What sort of life would you like to have after you get out of school? What are you interested in? What do you find worth doing? What is it that you love to do—what makes it seem as if time is flying by? It makes perfect sense that doing what you're good at and what gives you pleasure make your life more enjoyable. Take the time and make the effort to discover what you enjoy doing; then look for ways these activities could be applied to a career—and set some goals to check it out! Remember, the aim is to make your joys your job! Don't miss out on the chance to be really happy in your work—and in your life.

Taste-berry promise for the day: I will visit my school counselor and ask if there is a course or profile I can take to get a better idea of my personal strengths and aptitudes.

Give Yourself a Break

What's tough about getting to know yourself is that it's not just done in private: The world is watching!

Carrie Linn, 16
A Taste-Berry Teen's Guide to Managing the Stress and Pressures of Life

Do you feel "onstage" in the world? Do you feel as if all eyes are on you? You're out there in the world working on feeling great about yourself, but painfully aware that everyone else is watching you as you try to move gracefully through life. After all, there are times when navigating the fragile intricacies of daily life and its challenges that you feel as graceful as a rhino. You are just certain that everyone notices every time you mess up and is well aware of when you're having a bad-hair day. Don't let it beat up on your self-confidence. When you're having these feelings, remind yourself to stop. Give yourself a break: Take heart knowing that in spite of feeling like everyone is zeroed in on your every mishap and misstep, chances are they rarely even notice them. Concentrate on all your successes and laugh off your less sterling moments.

Taste-berry promise for the day: I will accept myself—warts and all.

Every Day Is a New Day

Say "yes" to life!

Jennifer Leigh Youngs
A Teen's Guide to Living Drug-Free

Looking out at the horizon at dawn, you see the sun, a fiery globe of shining light rising out of the fading darkness. With sunrise comes the promise of a new day. Every day is a new day, a chance to begin anew. A new day can be a taste berry that offers freedom from the darkness of the night it chased away. It can offer joy and new possibilities as you live it in the moment. Allow this day to be one that you wouldn't trade for any other. Be truly grateful for it and the fact that it is yours to live. Believe that you are worthy of sunrises, and then cherish them in each new day! All it takes is saying "yes" to life.

Taste-berry promise for the day: I will journal about the ways I am saying "yes" to life—and continue to say "yes" today!

Practice Forgiveness

> *The practice of forgiveness can be far nobler than the demand for justice.*

Brian Slamon, 16
More Taste Berries for Teens

When someone hurts you or does something "wrong," your first response may be, "He's going to pay!" You might even spend time and energy coming up with ways to get back at this person—certain that justice demands some sort of "payback." As Gandhi said, "If we practiced an eye for an eye, the world would all be blind." There is no time like the present to begin to seek a more peaceful solution in order to make the world a more loving and peaceful place. How do you seek peaceful solutions in your life? Treat others the way you want to be treated; respect their differences and use kind words often throughout your day. Don't worry that someone didn't get what he deserves, or that he doesn't know that you could really give it to him. Leave that up to a higher power to decide! Train your thoughts, attitudes and actions to focus on peaceful solutions.

Taste-berry promise for the day: I will call or write a letter to someone who I've been on "shaky terms" with and make an effort to come to a peaceful, forgiving solution.

Seek Your Higher Power

*B*elieving you can draw on the strength and power of
a loving and caring power—especially in your
darkest and most stressful moments—is the essence of
faith.

Bettie B. Youngs
A Taste-Berry Teen's Guide to Managing the Stress and Pressures of Life

Many people of all ages and backgrounds have found that
when they opened to the possibility of a loving, caring higher
power, they discovered that power was there to help them and
had been there for them all along. Acknowledging a one-on-one
relationship with a force greater than ourselves is the foundation
of faith. An unending source of strength, inner peace and guidance, this ever-available faith is an anchor that sustains us both
when things are going well and when we feel alone or overwhelmed. Believe that a loving, caring power is at work in the
world. Believe you can draw on this power and receive the end-
less taste berries of love, strength, peace and guidance that faith
offers.

Taste-berry promise for the day: I will make time
today to be alone and still, and feel the power of faith as I consider how it works in my life.

Discover Your Purpose

𝒲e humans are a soul-self, each on a journey in search of discovering purpose.

Bettie B. Youngs
A Teen's Guide to Living Drug-Free

Being together, talking, laughing and reminiscing—all are joyful, common experiences that affirm we are part of the greater whole of the human race. But though we are part of a massive human civilization, we are much like a single star among the vast galaxy—wherein each has its own force to play out. And though we each make the journey alongside others, we each experience things in our own way. As much as we enjoy exciting lives and good times with our friends and families, nothing takes the place of the search for the meaning and purpose of our own existence. Honor this quest: Do those things that inspire and uplift you and hold you to your highest good. Choose to be with those who treat you gently and lovingly, with great care and respect. Should you journey upon those who are not as yet enlightened to the importance of the soul-search, be kind, but tarry not. For your search is the one on which you must focus; others will choose to get on the road to their search when it is their time. Encourage them, but do not lose sight of your own mission—which is to discover the purpose and meaning of your own life.

Taste-berry promise for the day: I will honor the journey of my soul-self.

Live for Today

"*Just for today*" *is a great reminder to live in the present and not let myself get caught up in problems that haven't as yet arrived.*

Kyla Branson, 16
A Teen's Guide to Living Drug-Free

If you live your life worrying about all the "what ifs," racing ahead in your mind and fretting over everything that might go wrong tomorrow, you lose out on the wonder of the present day. And, of course, there is also the probability that you set yourself up for unhappiness with self-fulfilling prophecies of failure and disappointment. But if you just focus on the day at hand and do your best in it, you'll see that you can better handle it. Life is a series of *daily* victories and triumphs. When your life is manageable in the day at hand, it is therefore sweet enough.

Taste-berry promise for the day: I will live in the day.

"Snowball Control"

When you find yourself knee-deep in stress, it's best to start coping before it all snowballs—and buries you alive!

Rob Lawson, 15
A Taste-Berry Teen's Guide to Managing the Stress and Pressures of Life

When you're going through a stress-filled time—such as finals week or planning for some big event and hoping the date of your dreams asks you—it's important to make sure your stress doesn't get out of hand. Though you can't always control the situation, you can manage yourself—which can help you control your stress level. How do you keep stress from snowballing as one poorly managed situation collides into and creates yet another? You can decide to do "snowball control": You stay in the here and now and do what you have to do to deal with the stress going on right now in the moment. Remind yourself to relax, breathe and complete each task one by one, without running ahead and worrying about everything you need to do all at once. Follow this course of action, and you're sure to find that the snowball will slow its roll and then, like your stress level, it will slowly melt away!

Taste-berry promise for the day: I will make a checklist of all I have to do today—and then calmly focus on carrying out each task one at a time.

Love Is a Two-Way Street

*If you've recently steered into a one-way "love"
street, you'd better turn around and get out of it as
soon as possible!*

Lisa Morrison, 16
More Taste Berries for Teens

Have you ever been in a relationship that was really one-sided? No matter what side you were on, it didn't really feel right, did it? A healthy relationship is a two-way thing. Of course, in the beginning, we don't always know the other person: A relationship is about discovering more of what another person is like, his or her likes and dislikes, how he or she treats others and approaches life and so on. As you get to know someone, sometimes you find that this person is a really nice human being, and sometimes he or she turns out to be different than you thought—and not someone with whom you wish to spend your time. When this happens, you may have to rethink things—you may have to leave, especially if staying in the relationship means you have to compromise your values. Remember, love is a two-way street. Make certain both lanes are being traveled in your relationships.

Taste-berry promise for the day: I will spend time talking with and really getting to know someone who I think is special.

Believe and You Will Achieve

When you want to believe in something, you also have to believe in everything that's necessary for believing in it.

Hugo Bette, author
A Taste-Berry Teen's Guide to Setting & Achieving Goals

If you say you want to attend college, then you are going to have to do everything necessary to get into college, from getting the grades to meeting college entrance requirements, to believing that a college education will in some way improve your life. Do you want to believe in peace on the planet? Then you will have to do those things that show you are doing your part to be and to live that peace—which can mean showing acceptance not only to your friends, but all your classmates—and doing this not only with the cool kids, but also those you maybe think of as nerdy and yes, geeky, as well! When you believe in something, you have to believe in everything that breathes life into it, otherwise it will never come alive. What good do you believe in accomplishing? Commit to believing in all that's required to live that good.

Taste-berry promise for the day: I will have a meaningful conversation with someone who isn't in my circle of friends.

We Are Complex Beings

*T*he work of life is to grow closer to who we really are, closer to the image of the person we know our-selves to be.

Bettie B. Youngs
Taste Berries for Teens

We humans are multifaceted beings. There is the physical "you": You need to do certain things to have good health and to stay healthy. You are a social being: You are constantly wanting to interact with others. There is an intellectual side to you: You are a curious being, eager to gain more knowledge about the world around you and your place in it. And there is a spiritual side to you: that part of you that asks that you see yourself as sacred, a soul on its journey. In a very real sense then, we each know ourselves better than anyone else does. So much of the work of life is about balancing the "outside world" with the selves we already know. As you do the work of growing closer to the image of the person you know yourself to be, seek out those people and experiences that help you embrace the image you hold of yourself.

Taste-berry promise for the day: I will journal about the highest image I have of myself and how I can nurture it.

Reward Yourself

If you don't have a good PR firm, write your own press releases.

Jennifer Leigh Youngs
A Taste-Berry Teen's Guide to Setting & Achieving Goals

You identified what you wanted, you went out to get it and you got it. Reward yourself! Certainly having your name published in the school paper for an award you received or making the honor roll is wonderful recognition, as is earning a letter for your letter jacket. All indicate you are an achiever. Recognize yourself for a job well done! Whether you give yourself a new CD, buy Rollerblades or splurge on concert tickets, when you play the CD, go skating or look back on having been to the concert, you will connect it to the goal you achieved. Rewards are "press releases," reminders that you've applied yourself and have been successful. Bottom line: You're cool. You are a winner. Those reminders of how cool you are inspire you to keep on winning. Learn to give them to yourself—and don't forget to acknowledge others when they've announced a "win" as well.

Taste-berry promise for the day: I will reward myself for a job well done.

First Make a Decision

A decision is a very powerful act, because in essence, it's drawing a line, then stepping over to the other side. It's a vow.

Cassie Cable, 17
More Taste Berries for Teens

Have you ever heard someone say, "Once I'd made the decision, the rest was easy"? There is "magic" in the power of making a decision: It moves you to action. Deciding to act is your "yes" to going forward. But once you've "drawn the line," the action of "stepping over it" is required. When you decided you wanted to go out for sports, you packed your practice gear on mornings you had practice and showed up for practice whether you wanted to or not. You knew that "suiting up" and playing your best on game day required your diligence each and every practice session. Through action we learn and move forward in life. Make a decision to move toward your goals, and then take the action of each "step" needed to reach them.

Taste-berry promise for the day: I'll make a decision about an issue on which I've been sitting on the fence and take action on my goals.

Evaluate Your Values

I need a new life, a chance and a plan,
somewhere to build on rock, not sand.

Delilah Burton, 17
Taste Berries for Teens #3

Does your life feel out of sync with what you'd like it to be? Are you looking for more stability, but aren't sure how to find it? Do you feel as if you could use a new plan? Feeling stable or secure with yourself and your plan for your life starts with knowing what is most important to you. There may be times when you find you haven't stayed true to what you value—or when challenges have taken you to a place where you feel uncertain of everything. In these times, stop and reflect on what you value most. What is important to you? Safety? Security? Love? Honesty? Perseverance? Compassion? Self-esteem? These values can be the foundation for regrouping or rebuilding your life. This requires that you live your life according to them: If your value is honesty, in each situation ask, "What is the honest thing to do?" Then act according to your answer. Or if your value is self-esteem, ask, "What should I do in order to feel good about myself?" Or if it is love, ask, "What is the loving thing to do?" Whatever your values, allow them to guide you and give you a more secure foundation for "starting over."

Taste-berry promise for the day: I will talk with my best friend about values and how we are living up to our own.

Choose Your Actions and Reactions

I finally learned that when faced with consequences, I get to choose how I want to react. That insight has made a huge difference in my life.

Sara Jane Keller, 20
More Taste Berries for Teens

As you are learning, almost everything has a consequence—both positive and negative. Chances are by now you have experienced consequences. If you studied for a test, consequently you probably got a good grade. This was a "positive consequence"—but what about "negative consequences"? How do you deal with them? You can't always stop negative consequences, but you always get to choose how you will react to them. If you take responsibility for your role in them—if you weigh the consequences of your actions, both positive and negative—you'll find you're in a place of power. What happens to you in life is largely dependent on what choices you make. This is good news, as with most things, it means you can *choose* actions and reactions that lead to positive consequences.

Taste-berry promise for the day: I will act and react in ways that lead to positive consequences.

Listen to Your Feelings

$\mathscr{B}$eing around others is not only about gaining acceptance and fitting in, it's also about making decisions when it comes to the nature of others.

McKenna Jagger, 15
More Taste Berries for Teens

Your intuition speaks to you in the form of "feelings." Listen to what your instincts are telling you. If you have a friend who always seems to bring out the best in you, both intellect and intuition would agree it's a good relationship to nurture. If someone's actions clearly demonstrate a lack of respect for you, instincts would tell you that you should avoid that person's company when possible. If something in your heart, some "feeling," tells you someone is not what he appears to be, you would rightfully exercise caution around that person. Everyone wants to "fit in" and feel accepted, but be sure to listen to your intuition about who you allow yourself to "fit in" with. Your intuition, like your intelligence, is a gift meant to be used when making decisions on the nature of others. Don't ignore this taste berry of wisdom, protection and direction.

Taste-berry promise for the day: I will listen to my intuition.

We Are Many Selves

There's a me on the inside and a me on the out,
It's confusing us both, and keeps me in doubt ...
Inside and out! How long will it be
Before I'm together, and there's just one of me?

Mandy Flaspeter, 18
Taste Berries for Teens #3

One day do you feel as though you'd like to be a doctor and the next day a pro surfer? Do you want to dress like a rock star (and maybe be one)—but also like a "clean-cut All-American" look? One style appeals to you and then another—one look, one career, one future—then yet another still. It can all seem very confusing! Take heart: Such duplicities are perfectly normal. These "many selves"—doctor, surfer, rock star, All-American and the entire cast of characters and aspirations—will one day reconcile, and you will be certain of and comfortable with who you are. Today, accept that within you hold all these possibilities. Explore them wisely and delight in discovering which is best for you.

Taste-berry promise for the day: I will journal about all the many sides of me and what each means to me.

Have a Beautiful Day!

Another beautiful day, and one filled with such possibilities!

Alma Russ, 18
Feeling Great, Looking Hot & Loving Yourself! Health, Beauty and Fitness for Teens

Have you ever gotten up in the morning, looked out your window and your first words were, "What a beautiful day!" Or anticipating your plans, have you said, "All right! I've got such a great day ahead of me!" When you are grateful and simply saying thank you for life and for being, your heart is open: Open to beauty, open to others, open for opportunities and all that is good. As you listen closely to the gratitude as it whispers to your heart of the beauty and the good, don't forget to thank the source of all that perfection.

Taste-berry promise for the day: I will look at the beauty in this day and be grateful for it.

You Can Do It!

> *eep your eyes on the goal, believing in your ability to reach it. When doubt sets in, walk through your fears by placing one foot in front of the other.*

Jennifer Leigh Youngs
A Taste-Berry Teen's Guide to Setting & Achieving Goals

Have you ever wanted to achieve a certain goal so much that the thought of not being able to actually scared you? Did you want to pass an important test or make it on a team, and thinking you might fail, you felt fearful? Did you want to go out with someone special, and the fear that that person might say no stopped you from asking at all? This happens to all of us. It can help to remind yourself that when doubt sets in, the balancing pole of belief in yourself can remain firmly in your hands. Be persistent: Just keep putting one foot in front of the other, taking the next required action until you reach your destination. Believe in yourself; you can do it!

Taste-berry promise for the day: I will believe in myself.

Expect the Best in Relationships

Having a special someone in your life should not mean that you have to give up being you.

Jennifer Leigh Youngs
Taste Berries for Teens #3

The "perfect" love has come along, and you're swept away by the wonder of it. But just because you've found the special someone of your dreams doesn't mean nothing else in your world matters or that you stop enjoying time with your friends. It doesn't mean that other things in your life come to a halt, such as time with your family or your focus on doing well in school or getting to your job on time. Keep an eye on what you change and how and why you make changes for a friend or someone special. What if you find yourself having gone too far in your compromises and you want to "return to yourself"? Let the other person know what matters to you—if you haven't shared these things, they can't be known. Both you and the other person are deserving of a good, healthy relationship. Don't settle for less.

Taste-berry promise for the day: I will expect the best in my relationships.

Value Differences

We can dance a dance to the music of our own making, and still come together where, like petals embracing the sun, we open knowingly.

Jennifer Leigh Youngs
Taste Berries for Teens #3

Those times when you honestly connect with a person you love can literally change your life. To know that your love is assured even when you completely bare your heart and soul grants you a greater depth of security that can give you new levels of confidence. Being able to trust another person in this way is such a great gift. What a wonderful knowing: On our journey, there are those who make it safe for us to bare our souls and allow our natures to bloom—even when their dance and its music are very different from our own. What a loving, taste-berry-like gesture!

Taste-berry promise for the day: I will tell one of my parents why I appreciate both our love and our differences.

Little Things Matter

oing things like building a hospital are, of course, awesome work, but I believe that doing the small day-to-day work with the same sort of dedication can make as big a difference in the world.

Merrilee Moens, 16
More Taste Berries for Teens

Take a moment to sincerely reflect on why you love the people who mean the most to you in life—whether your friends, your parents, your grandparents or a special someone. Which of their words and actions stir those feelings of love in you most? With honest reflection, you'll likely find it's the small things they do and say each day to show you that they care that mean the most to you. Of course, the great gestures of love—whether on special occasions or in a crisis—mean a lot, too. But when you take a deeper look at the matter, it's their caring about you that inspires your love the most. It's a good model for making a difference in the world: It, too, is done in the daily sharing of our love for others.

Taste-berry promise for the day: I will think about three ways I make a positive difference in the lives of others.

Nurture Your Soul

It's good to remind ourselves that we are "spiritual beings having a human experience."

Bettie B. Youngs
A Teen's Guide to Living Drug-Free

Take a moment to reflect on who you are: You have a body and a mind, but when you honestly reflect on it, aren't you quite certain that "who you are" is much more than your body and even more than your mind? When you take the time to contemplate it, don't you find that there is something greater within you that more fully defines and identifies you? This is sometimes called the soul—and sometimes known as the spiritual aspect of being "you." We would do well to remember this deeper essence or identity, and to nurture and care for it. This nurturing is done by establishing a one-on-one relationship with a higher power, by taking the time to connect with the source of that spirit within. Ask for this connection, do the footwork of searching, keep an open mind and heart—and faith, hope and love will nourish the deepest part of you.

Taste-berry promise for the day: I will look into the mirror and ask myself, "Who am I?"—and reflect on my answer.

Help Someone Feel Terrific

I've discovered that people who are generous with helping you feel "terrific" are those who are really secure within themselves.

Bradley Dawson, 17
Taste Berries for Teens

Think of someone who believes you're a terrific person. What kind of things do they say to you? Can you see a sparkle in their eyes when they look at you? Doesn't it feel great to be around them? Whether a grandparent, friend, parent or brother or sister, when you spend time with someone who thinks you're terrific, it's sure to make you feel like you are just that. Few things are greater for your sense of feeling loved, as well as for your success in life. When someone believes in you, it brings you that much closer to being successful in the things you do, because it helps you believe in yourself, too. Knowing what a great gift it is to have someone believe in you this way, make certain that you give this gift of "belief" to others. Go ahead, be secure—help someone else feel like a "terrific" person.

Taste-berry promise for the day: I will tell my family members why I think they're terrific.

Goals Are Stepping-Stones

Your goals are stepping-stones that move you toward your ultimate dream.

Bettie B. Youngs
A Taste-Berry Teen's Guide to Setting & Achieving Goals

Have you ever made your way across a creek? Glancing to where you'd like to end up at the other shore, you hop from one stepping-stone to the next, each one bringing you closer to the other side. It's the same process in reaching your goals. Daily goals connect you to your weekly goals connecting you to your monthly goals connecting you to your yearly goals. Goals are all stepping-stones for getting you closer to your destination—your ultimate dream. Yet unlike the stepping-stones of a creek whose placement is at nature's whim, those that bridge you to your dreams are yours to put in place. What are your goals? How many "stepping-stones" are needed to get where you're headed?

Taste-berry promise for the day: I will share with a friend or family member what my goals are and what I think it will take for me to reach them.

Let Your Parents Know You Love Them

Little children step on your feet; big children step on your heart.

Bettie B. Youngs
Taste Berries for Teens #3

How many ways do your parents show their love for you? How do they let you know how much they care? Do they try to set up guidelines to protect you? Do they say "I love you" in words as well as actions? We can sometimes take for granted those who are always there for us, especially in the teen years when there's such a desire for more independence. When you don't let your parents know that you love them, you "step on their hearts." So remember to let your parents know everything you appreciate about them. Be their taste berry: Thank them for the ways they demonstrate their love for you.

Taste-berry promise for the day: I will let my parents know I appreciate them.

Live in Your Heart Daily

I knew someone who lived in her heart daily. It was an awesome experience. I'd like to do the same.

Anika Aviara, 16
More Taste Berries for Teens

What does it mean to "live in your heart daily"? It means to live your life from a place of love and compassion. It means to see life and circumstance from the eyes of your heart. When you live from this place, there is little room for petty judgments and criticisms, or for prejudice and superficial attitudes. To live in your heart daily is to be a "taste berry" to each person that you meet, in your home, in your school, in your community, in your world. To live in your heart is to consciously live with love in each moment. Do you know someone who lives in her heart—your mom or dad, or one of your teachers who lived in her heart, since so many of them do? Would your friends describe you as someone who lives in her heart?

Taste-berry promise for the day: I will see life from the eyes of my heart.

Love Makes the World Beautiful

Love changes everything.

E.K.H., 17
More Taste Berries for Teens

Have you ever "fallen in love"? Didn't the world suddenly seem like a more beautiful place? In fact, didn't everyone seem to be more likable, as well? It isn't just romantic love that can shade your world with brighter hues. All love has this power. Love's magic is that it takes you out of yourself and helps you see the rest of the world. If you adore your pet, chances are, you readily see animals and are fond of them. If you love that you are a close family unit, chances are, when you see another family together, you smile knowingly. When you are in a place of love, your focus expands beyond just yourself and into a greater interest and care for others. All people and all life seem to have more meaning and greater purpose. Be love's taste berry: Balance thoughts of self with sincere interest and concern for others.

Taste-berry promise for the day: I will identify all the ways I am a loving person.

Choose to Be Positive

When you touch the lives of others—when you help make their lives brighter and better—you make your own brighter and better, as well.

Steve Hand, 16
Taste Berries for Teens

Have you ever made a decision to be positive, to make every word out of your mouth uplifting and to do your very best all day? Did you notice how good it made you feel? Didn't you have more patience and more tolerance for everyone around you? If you go through the day saying things that are inspiring and putting your very best into the things that you do, you'll most likely feel uplifted and get the best out of the things that you do. And, what you say and do as you move through your day can have a true impact on others. Choose to be positive, uplifting and uplifted; choose to do and get the best in this day.

Taste-berry promise for the day: I will practice saying only positive things and put my best into everything I do today.

Give Yourself a Pep Talk

When you look in the mirror, encourage yourself:
Pep talks are always welcome!

Jennifer Leigh Youngs
Taste Berries for Teens #3

Have you ever given yourself a pep talk in the mirror? If not, it's time to start! You wouldn't think of running into a good friend and not stopping to exchange words of encouragement and support. Be as good to yourself as you are to your friends. Tell yourself how good you're doing and all the ways you're right on target in your life, and, of course, how cool you are. Say all those encouraging, uplifting things you'd love to hear from someone else. Did someone forget to tell you "thanks" for doing something special? Next time you're having a "face-to-face," you can make up for that person's oversight: You can thank *you!* Rallying around yourself will help give you all the confidence you need to tackle your challenges with grace. Perhaps even more important, the more you learn to love the face in the mirror, the better you'll love everyone else in your life.

Taste-berry promise for the day: I'll have a talk with the face in the mirror on a daily basis.

Throw Away the "What Ifs"

Instead of focusing on the negatives and the "what ifs," focus on what you can do to change the situation in a positive way.

Bettie B. Youngs
Taste Berries for Teens Journal

Have you ever been caught up in a brainstorm of reviewing everything that went wrong in a situation—detailing all the things you "could've or should've" said differently, all the different ways you "could've or should've" handled it from beginning to end? You can become so caught up in the past (which you can't change), that you aren't able to change the present. But when you focus on what you can do right in the "here and now" to create positive change, there is hope of the change being realized. Begin by "rewriting" the way you think about the situation—get back in charge by concentrating on how you can change things for the better today.

Taste-berry promise for the day: I will write about what action I can take right now to create the change I want to see.

Set Limits in Love

You can give too much or go too far in the name of love.

Christopher Gillian, 17
Taste Berries for Teens

Love is so important to feeling whole and connected to others. Because love is so essential to us, it's worth protecting—which includes setting limits. Setting limits doesn't mean that you are less loving or less loveable; it means just the opposite—you are loveable and worth loving. Love doesn't ask that you give up your values, compromise your integrity or endanger your self-respect—it asks that you safeguard them. You set boundaries to preserve these qualities. Have you set boundaries for the way you will allow yourself to be treated in a relationship? Have you set boundaries for how much you will give—and how much you will take? These boundaries are the framework of a truly loving relationship: They assure that you are both loving and being true to yourself, so you are able to love and give honestly to others. Determine what you feel is "too much" and "too far" in the name of love, and then set your boundaries accordingly.

Taste-berry promise for the day: I will think about what is really important to me and consider if I've set boundaries to protect those values.

Mistakes Mean You're Human

Accept that you're human—and are therefore capable of great deeds—and great blunders.

Bettie B. Youngs
Taste Berries for Teens #3

You are capable of great acts of love, accomplishment and understanding—and you are just as capable of blunders and unfortunate mistakes. Mistakes or shortcomings are simply part of the package when it comes to being human. To expect anything other than this mix of greatness and imperfection is not wise: If you don't allow for the occasional mistakes, you're sure to feel disappointed when they happen. If you don't expect the acts of greatness, you may well fail to step up to them when the opportunity presents itself. Holding onto this realistic image of yourself can bring you both greater acceptance and greater achievement. These are two great gifts, for both acceptance and achievement are a dynamic combination in a life of great success. Practice these taste berries and claim new victories both in your life and your view of yourself.

Taste-berry promise for the day: I will talk over my mistakes with a safe friend and then let them go once and for all.

Conserve Earth's Resources

Everything we do, good or bad, makes a difference to every living thing, as well as to the universe and all its planets.

Brian Lumke, 12
Taste Berries for Teens

Our actions can have a sort of domino effect on all living things: The paper you use on both sides conserves the timberlands, which in turn saves the forests needed for converting our carbon dioxide into oxygen, which in turn is the air we breathe in order to survive. Learn to respect all living things. Each day, practice doing what you can to make a difference to all life on this planet. Collectively we can heal, nourish and make a difference. Be a taste berry: Do your part.

Taste-berry promise for the day: I will think about five ways I can conserve the Earth's resources.

Practice Acts of Kindness

Time fades memories, but it never fades the joy you feel when you've done something thoughtful for another.

Mike Siciliano, 15
Taste Berries for Teens

Doing something nice for someone gives you a genuine sense of purpose and joy. When you do something good for someone else, it continues to live on in your memory. No one can take that act of kindness away from you. It nourishes your spirit and your soul, just as it feeds the heart of the other person. Take a moment to reflect on the good you were able to share with someone else. Allow the memory to give you a lift, to boost your view of yourself and of the purpose of your life. Vow to live your life with such deeds.

Taste-berry promise for the day: I will go through the family photo album with members of my family and reminisce about all the good we've shared.

Day 301

Honor Your Teachers

When things get tough for me, I get out my annual and read what one of my favorite teachers wrote: "You have great promise! I hope you'll work hard, go to a fine university and help change the world. If ever you doubt yourself, just remember that I believe in you!"

Lana Bowman, 17
Taste Berries for Teens

Who is your favorite teacher—and why? Which teacher made the greatest impact on your life, or have there been so many that it's hard to narrow it down to just one? Teachers affect our lives in so many important ways: By believing in you, they can inspire you to believe in yourself. Sharing their years of experience and knowledge, they educate you in academics that have the potential to carry you into your future, to connect you with your passions and to motivate you to go on to greater levels of learning. Through demonstration, their dedication and creativity, and their patience and compassion teach you lessons no planned curriculum can offer. Honor all those great teachers who have so generously acted as taste berries in your life, whether educators, parents, friends, or those life lessons that have effected positive growth and helped you become who you are today.

Taste-berry promise for the day: I will thank my favorite teacher for all the ways he or she has touched my life.

The Sooner the Better

If you don't set goals for yourself, expect your life to be dull, "same-old, same-old," and totally boring!

Craig Santos, 18
A Taste-Berry Teen's Guide to Setting & Achieving Goals

Probably you know exactly where you're heading: You know where you want to go to college, what sort of a job or career you'd like, maybe you've even thought about where you want to live or what sort of "lifestyle" you'd like to have. This is good. If you want to have a "totally" interesting and rewarding life, you've got to think about what's important to you, and then set goals to turn your aspirations into reality. The sooner, the better. The sooner you start saving money to buy a car, the easier it will be to own one on the day you'd like to have it. The sooner you start working toward getting good grades, the better chance you'll have of securing a good grade point average. The sooner you think about creating "something handmade" as a unique gift for an upcoming occasion for a special someone, the more likely it is you'll have it ready in time to present it to that person. It's never too early to make your life as exciting as you'd like it to be!

Taste-berry promise for the day: I'll make a "to-do" list of all of the things I need to accomplish today.

Wear a Smile

*N*ever frown because you never know who is falling in
love with your smile.

Jennifer Leigh Youngs
More Taste Berries for Teens

Is there someone whose smile just melts your heart? Have you
ever seen your best friend's smile from down the halls at school
and felt instantly brighter? Can you remember a time your parent's smile from the bleacher of a game or the seats of the school
theater or auditorium brought you courage? Don't you love to
see sincere smiles? Such smiles have the power to make you feel
welcome, safe, happy and less alone. When you see someone
smile at you, it's natural to smile in return. You can just "feel" a
smile with your heart. This makes perfect sense, since a smile is
an expression of the heart complete with the power to dazzle
and comfort others—perhaps, to the point of falling in love with
you! It has been said that smiles are food for the heart, or as
Joseph Addison said: "What sunshine is to flowers, smiles are to
humanity." Sincere smiles express gratitude for the moment—
and for those who are part of it. Share this gratitude with your
smile—it's sure to make you feel a greater sense of belonging on
the planet.

Taste-berry promise for the day: I will promote joy by
sharing a joyful smile.

Recover from Setbacks

Success is not measured by your victories as much as by how you recover from your failures.

Vic Preisser
More Taste Berries for Teens

Think back on those times you bounced back from some tough break: Maybe a low grade in a class meant you were cut from a sports team. Though devastated, you decided you were going to turn things around. You worked really hard, brought up the grade and were back on the team the very next season. Recovering from a setback is in itself a victory—all the more rewarding since by its very nature it was hard won—but it is even more than a victory. It is a true measure of success. When you put your all into moving forward, into recovering from setbacks, you show facets of your character that might not be revealed otherwise: determination, perseverance, courage, faith in your goals and confidence in yourself. Let setbacks be a measure of "real" successes.

Taste-berry promise for the day: I will look at my recent setback and build a plan with specific steps I can take to help move me in a new direction.

Let Your Eyes Sparkle with Kindness

There's nothing more radiant than an inner harmony that displays itself in the sparkling eyes of someone who is generous enough to care about others.

Jennifer Leigh Youngs
Feeling Great, Looking Hot & Loving Yourself! Health, Fitness and Beauty for Teens

Have you seen someone whose eyes spoke volumes about how much they loved life—or you? Have you looked at someone and you could just tell this was a genuinely kind person who really cared about others? Has someone ever made eye contact with you in a way that spoke of comfort when you were feeling sad, or joy when you were feeling happy? As the saying goes, "Eyes are the windows to the soul." Our eyes tell the story of how we're feeling: Whatever is in your heart will radiate in your eyes. Do your eyes speak and sparkle with kindness? Be in love with life, and it's sure to show up in the sparkle of your eyes.

Taste-berry promise for the day: I will look into the mirror and see what my eyes are showing others about how happy I am with myself—and with life.

Do Your Part for Peace

*W*hat an amazingly simple concept: Peace begins with each person.

Maylynn Lingh, 16
Taste Berries for Teens #3

There are many simple ways to promote peace in your day-to-day life. Have you ever been with friends when one of them starts talking about someone you all know, putting down this other person and listing all his or her "faults"? You could always join in and make some criticism, as well. But you could also point out some "saving grace" about this person, or say something that might make your friends think about how unkind their comments are—in essence, you could help them put themselves in check. Of course, remaining silent is another option. Which option would you choose if you were committed to doing your part to create and keep peace in the world and within your heart? Be a taste berry: Do those things that create peace within you and on the planet. Apply this standard to every issue, every day and to every person. Peace is an attitude: Think it, love it, live it.

Taste-berry promise for the day: I will make a collage with the theme of peace and hang it in my room to remind me to live in peaceful ways.

Look for the Pearl

Consider how a beautiful pearl is the outcome of an intrusion (such as a grain of sand) within the oyster's shell. Likewise, the intrusion of disappointment, heartache or a particularly difficult time can transform a person into an illustrious soul.

Bettie B. Youngs
More Taste Berries for Teens

Inevitably each of us will face times of sadness, sorrow or challenge in our lives—whether in the form of heartbreak, disappointment, humiliation, loss or other struggles. But we must celebrate the challenge as an opportunity to gain strength from its lesson and not dwell solely on the source of our pain. What the process of the development of a pearl teaches us is that suffering can be transformed into the pearl of renewed courage, hope, endurance, wisdom, faith or love. Each is a testimony of the majesty of the heart and soul to use sad times to deepen into life—to more fully appreciate our own resilience. Trust that you can learn something even in the challenge—and look for the pearl you have gained.

Taste-berry promise for the day: I will remind myself that the source of strength comes from facing each day's realities.

Music Can Change Your Mood

*M*usic is a powerful influence on your moods and attitudes! So, when you're stressed out, plug in some
mellow music and let it calm you down.

Amanda Martinez, 16
A Taste-Berry Teen's Guide to Managing the Stress and Pressures of Life

Music is, well, ear candy! And here's more sweet news: Music
has the power to transform just about any mood you're in! Have
you ever put on one of your favorite CDs and then found yourself dancing around the room, feeling yourself filled with joy and
playfulness? Have you ever put on music that made you calm,
tired, energized, melancholy, cheerful, sad or put you in a great
mood? Music has the power to transform the way you feel.
Soothing music can relieve your stress by helping you relax,
even lull you to sleep. So especially when you're stressed out,
use music to help you calm down. Turn on some positive and
upbeat music to give you energy and get you going in the morning. Music: What a taste berry! It not only can sweeten a sour
day, but it can improve our attitude as well!

Taste-berry promise for the day: I will listen to a song
that makes me feel like dancing.

Ask for Help

*W*e are each responsible for the decisions and choices *we make, but that doesn't mean that two heads aren't better than one.*

Sam Murray, 15
Taste Berries for Teens

There can be so many decisions that ultimately are up to each of us, and yet there are occasions when advice or support is needed—everything from choosing a college or career, to what to do when a classmate is using alcohol or drugs. Fortunately, we need only look around to discover that we are not on the journey of life alone! We are supposed to help and assist one another. Seeking counsel shows that you are wise. When you are in need of direction or support, don't hesitate to ask for it. Reach out to those taste berries who are both willing and able to sweeten your life.

Taste-berry promise for the day: I will make a list of the top five people I can go to for advice.

The Transforming Power of Love

We *all have the ability to bring the transforming*
power of love into our lives: It can be as simple as
giving love.

Jennifer Leigh Youngs
More Taste Berries for Teens

Do you remember someone being there to hug you when your heart hurt? Didn't it soothe the ache? Was there a time when all you could do to help someone was to offer the fact that you really cared and your shoulder for them to cry on? Whether the person was a friend with a broken heart or a cranky toddler you were baby-sitting, no doubt your loving care truly made a difference. Sometimes just being there to love another person has the power to transform and heal that person's pain. If you don't have the words, and you don't know what to do, just share your support; love alone can lend strength. Love has a power beyond words and actions; sincerely given, even with your silent presence, it can bolster and comfort, uplift and transform. And here's the other side of the taste berry of love: While giving it, you'll find you are also being touched and transformed by it, as it creates new depths of compassion and feelings of connection in your heart.

Taste-berry promise for the day: I will hug someone who could use some cheering up.

Let Your Personality Shine

You'll be much happier working at a job or career that allows your personality to shine for what it is.

Colette Feener, 16
A Taste-Berry Teen's Guide to Setting & Achieving Goals

What is it that allows your personality to shine—is it when you're speaking to a large group of people or when you're talking one-on-one? Does your personality best shine when you're talking about one particular subject in school or an interest you have outside of school? Does it perk up when you're listening to others or when you're making them laugh? Is it brighter when you're with people or with animals? Do you prefer doing things inside, or are you happiest when outside in the elements, such as playing sports or doing yard work? Consider when your personality is "most happy." When you have your answer, you'll have a map to lead you to the kind of work that will bring you joy. It's yours for the search. Don't miss the opportunity to build your future around the jewel of who you really are.

Taste-berry promise for the day: I will make a list of those times when my personality "best shines."

Selfless Expressions of Love

Being a good person isn't only about being kind and nice, but rather, serving and caring for each other.

Kate Harmon, 18
Taste Berries for Teens #3

Perhaps the purest of all gifts is the one given with absolutely no thought of gain, nor any desire to feel virtuous. Such gifts are the fruit of a love that is based on a soul-deep recognition of our oneness as human beings. Selfless expressions of love are so profound, even when these gestures look simple, even basic: an arm of comfort around someone else's shoulder when it's clear to you that person is feeling down; reassuring words to someone who appears to be upset. Caring for others is what being a taste berry is all about—giving freely from your heart. Practice this kind of simple generosity.

Taste-berry promise for the day: I will ask someone what I can do to help and be ready to do so.

Make a New Plan

Don't let a failure throw you off course. Should you "bomb out" at something, regroup, make a new plan and begin again. It really is that simple!

Kevin Tulane, 17
Taste Berries for Teens Journal

Have you ever "bombed out" at something? To fail at something isn't such a great feeling: You can and should expect that you'll feel "down" and "low" for a little while. But know that failure is not the end of the world; you'll survive and can even thrive through those times you don't succeed. The important thing is to not be down on yourself for long. Give yourself a little time to "get over it." Think about why things didn't work out as you'd planned, make a new plan and then move on. You have other things to do; it's a big world out there—don't keep everyone waiting!

Taste-berry promise for the day: I will list three successes I've had this week.

Make a Difference Right at Home

I want my life to have made a difference in the world.

Merrilee Moens, 16
More Taste Berries for Teens

How do you think you can make a difference in the world? Would you like to go to a third-world country and help feed the poor? Maybe you see yourself working with some sort of organization for inner-city youth? Perhaps it is some other vision of social or humanitarian work you envision. When thinking of "making a difference" in the world, often thoughts turn to changing the world "out there" far away from home. But the truth is you don't have to go anywhere: Making a difference can begin right at home—with your friends and family; within your school and neighborhood. In fact, it's possible to make a true difference in the lives of those with whom you spend the most time. They see you every day, and the opportunities to share and show how much you care are always present. Support and uplift those you love, and you will make a difference in their lives—and in the world.

Taste-berry promise for the day: I will help someone I love finish his or her chores.

Make Your Dreams Come True

$\mathcal{D}$o what it takes today to live your dreams tomorrow.

Jennifer Leigh Youngs
A Taste-Berry Teen's Guide to Setting & Achieving Goals

What will it take to make your dreams come true? It's important to believe in yourself when you set out to make your dreams come true—and you're sure to boost your belief in yourself if you're diligent in doing all that you can to achieve success. If your goal is to get an A on your history test, be prepared for the test. Of course, this means study, study, study, as well as making sure you get the sleep and nourishment you need to be at your best when you take the test. If your goal is to backpack through Europe the summer after you graduate, there will be goals to set in motion to make sure you're ready when the day is at hand. Maybe your goal is even more long-term, like your dream for a career that requires a college degree—there is work to do today in reaching that goal for the future. What are you doing today to make your dreams come true?

Taste-berry promise for the day: I will write down all the goals I have to meet to make my dreams come true.

The Need to Change

When you find yourself at a crossroads, you really should check to see that there are no semi-trucks coming before you proceed!

Adam Mason, 16
A Teen's Guide to Living Drug-Free

Can you think of a time when you were at a crossroads in your life? Was there a time when you were living in a way that didn't serve your best interests? When you were settling for something less or going along with what others valued? Didn't something inside call to you—demanding that you change? You can reach a point in your life when you just know that you are off course— a point where you sense there is a semi-truck of disaster heading straight for you. Do you need to change? The best place to start is with your decision: "Today is the day that I change my life and do those things that move me toward a more honest expression of who I am." Take some time to reflect on the changes you want to create in yourself. What is it that expresses who you are and the values you hold dear? What changes can you make in order to live in alignment with this person and these values? Day by day be your own taste berry and live according to those changes.

Taste-berry promise for the day: I will tell my best friend what changes I am committed to making.

Be There for Others

How happy everyone in the world could be ... if only we would encourage and comfort each other.

Bill Lempke, 15
More Taste Berries for Teens

When we encourage and comfort each other along the journey of life, we create a sense of community, the feeling that we care and look out for each other. Knowing there are others who have our best interests at heart makes us all feel safer. When we demonstrate our willingness to entwine our lives, a powerful sense of interdependence is created. The feeling that each of us will "be there" for the other—that we are willing to be our "brother's keeper"—can help us feel that we are not alone: We can trust each other. Such is a source of comfort for citizens the world over. Ask yourself, "How can I look out for my best interests as well as the best interests of others today?"

Taste-berry promise for the day: I will do something kind to "be there" for someone else.

Happiness Is a Decision

Being a happy person was a decision I made and not something that happened to me.

Todd Larkin, 16
Taste Berries for Teens #3

You get out of bed in the morning, look around and think, "It's another day. Same as yesterday, same for tomorrow: school, soccer practice after school, dinner, homework, chores, bed." Are you happy? Probably you can't imagine the importance of the question until you know what it takes for you to be happy. But here's the thing: Happiness isn't "out there"—it's a decision you make. It's an attitude you carry within. How you view yourself and your world is entirely up to you. This is very good news: If you don't like the view, choose a new one! Every day you have a new chance to choose to be happy, to see the good in your world, to accept the miracle of your life. Choose to celebrate your life and all the good in it. Choose to be a happy person, and the taste berry of happiness will "happen" to you.

Taste-berry promise for the day: I will choose a song that makes me happy to play or sing at those times when I'm feeling "blah."

Cultivate Healthy Relationships

I love you not only because of who you are, but because of "who I am" when I am with you.

Bettie B. Youngs
Taste Berries for Teens Journal

Does being in a relationship with your special someone cause you to be more warm and wonderful? Do you have friends who seem to always bring out your best? This is how it should be. Feeling loved can help us to be better and more positive people. Some relationships just seem to nurture and inspire us to be more loving, kind, compassionate and wise. On the other hand, there may also be relationships that lead us to be moodier, more frustrated, upset or angry. This is one reason why it is so important to think carefully about the person who you allow to become your special someone—as well as those you choose as friends. Once you are in relationships, it's also a good reason to make sure they remain healthy. Continue to ask yourself: "How does my being with this person make me feel about myself?" and, "Do I appreciate 'who I am' when I am with this person?" If the answers are less than taste-berry league, think about making a change.

Taste-berry promise for the day: I will take inventory of how I feel about myself in all my relationships.

Believe in Yourself!

Sometimes the "leap" you have to take is one of faith—faith in yourself.

Jennifer Leigh Youngs
Taste Berries for Teens

What's your greatest challenge in life? Can you picture yourself overcoming that challenge? What is your greatest dream? Can you picture yourself living that dream? Are you certain that you have "what it takes" to make it happen? The ability to believe in yourself can help you accomplish great things, whether overcoming obstacles or reaching for the stars. It gives you crucial "You can do it!" confidence. Although, of course, we hope to have others to cheer us on in life, the most valuable cheerleader of all is the one who is with you literally all of the time—you. Not only are there those times when you're all alone, but unfortunately there are also those days when others may not believe in you. Never underestimate your own power to succeed—or the importance of believing that you can. Ask yourself, "What can I do today to build faith and confidence in myself?"

Taste-berry promise for the day: I will make a poster charting all my victories through the year.

Set Goals

There is a difference between "wishing, wanting and hoping" and making your dreams come true. Setting goals is the key.

Bettie B. Youngs
A Taste-Berry Teen's Guide to Setting & Achieving Goals

Finding out what you're about—what you're most interested in doing, being and having—is a most important discovery. But in order to bring your hopes and aspirations into being, you'll need to set goals and make a plan for accomplishing them. The difference between those who hope for things and those who bring them about (or are on their way to bringing them about) is having goals. So after you've identified what goals you find worthy, make a plan so that you begin to work toward achieving them. Feeling that you're making strides toward accomplishing those things you'd like to "do, have and be" is a good feeling—and an empowering one. Make those strides.

Taste-berry promise for the day: I will take one action to move me closer to what I want to do, have and be.

Create Miracles

Being a taste berry is the way to become the source of your own miracles.

Jennifer Leigh Youngs
More Taste Berries for Teens

What is a miracle? Miracles are transformations. A simple seed blossoms into a beautiful flower. A person can have a shift in his or her thinking and become totally changed for the better. These sorts of changes, these transformations, are in themselves a brand of miracles. How do you create miracles for others? Look for ways to support and encourage them. After all, helping others has the potential to create change or transformations in their lives. How does this become the source of miracles in your own life, too? The meaning, the love expressed, expands your sense of yourself as someone who matters. Turning your focus outward, moving from "me" to "you," makes your life richer and happier and hence becomes the source of miracles for others—and for you.

Taste-berry promise for the day: I will share words of hope with someone else.

Faith Flavors Your Days

F̃aith is the wellspring from which hope, peace and love flow.

Bettie B. Youngs
More Taste Berries for Teens

Belief and trust in an infinite loving power and presence are the essence of faith. Imagine the peace and comfort of believing that there is a power greater than you that is always there for you—unconditionally and constantly available and present. Imagine the strength and hope in trusting that this power loves and cares for you no matter what, always and forever. Imagine the sense of gratitude this knowledge would inspire and the love within you it would create. Does the taste berry of faith sweeten your days? Allow yourself to experience it.

Taste-berry promise for the day: I will take time to quietly consider what faith means to me.

Spend Precious Time Wisely

I don't want to waste another minute moving away from who it is I want to become. My goal is to make up for lost time.

Sara Jane Keller, 20
More Taste Berries for Teens

Do you make the most of your days? Do you do those things that help you reach your goals and bring you closer to who you are and who you would like to become? Can you recall a period of time that you now feel as if you wasted—time you feel you've lost to poor choices, like doing drugs or compromising your values for the sole reason of being accepted by someone else? In avoiding such choices, it can be helpful to review the way you live each day. At the end of the day, are you able to look back over it with satisfaction, knowing and believing that your time was well spent? You've probably heard that "life is precious"— are you a faithful caretaker of this gift? If not, starting today give yourself 365 taste berries of days well-spent.

Taste-berry promise for the day: I will make a schedule of all I want to do to make the most of my day.

Day 325

Let Others "Hold Your Heart"

While hurting is a personal "pain" for each of us, we need not go through it alone.

Tina Moreno
A Teen's Guide to Living Drug-Free

Have you ever had your heart broken but didn't want anyone to see how much it hurt you? Perhaps your family was going through a crisis of some sort, and you felt like you had to keep your "family problems" and how much they upset you a secret. Or, maybe you didn't make the cut on a certain school team, or you lost your campaign for student office and didn't want anyone to know how devastated you felt. Have you ever been betrayed by a friend, but you didn't want anyone to see you cry over it—because you were embarrassed or just afraid to be vulnerable? Often the land of tears feels as if it is meant to be a private place. But you don't have to suffer alone. The wiser and more honest decision is to let others know you are hurting and to allow them to "hold your heart" as you make it past your pain. Not only does this give them the opportunity to be a taste berry in your life, but as you're comforted and supported, you see and feel the importance of comforting and supporting others, as well.

Taste-berry promise for the day: I will let others know when I need support.

Be a Good Friend

A *true friend is someone who reaches for your hand and touches your heart.*

Jillian Sanderson, 17
Taste Berries for Teens #3

Have you ever had a friend who reached out to "be there" for you? If so, you know how much her acceptance—her outstretched hand—touched your heart. It showed you that she cared. It demonstrated her willingness to stand by you and support you. Feeling accepted inspires friendship, confidence and gratitude. Are you an understanding friend? Do you reach out to "be there" for others? Ask yourself, "How can I offer my friends the taste berry of genuine care and acceptance?"

Taste-berry promise for the day: I will tell my friends how much I care about them.

Walk Away—From Bad Company

*T*he worst way to miss someone is to be sitting right beside them knowing you can't "reach" them.

Delia Anne McNaughton, 17
A Teen's Guide to Living Drug-Free

Have you ever had a friend who is making painful mistakes—but won't listen to your warnings? Is there someone who you've talked to until you feel as if there's nothing more that you can say, but that person just keeps on making the same destructive choices over and over again? It can be frustrating to watch someone you care about do this. You really want to help! But it's important to remember that God doesn't need any of us to police the universe. Treating someone with compassion is much more apt to inspire them to change. Communicate with kindness and honesty—without judging and lecturing. After you have done this, keep in mind that "change" begins with you—maybe it's not wise for you to stay in this person's company. Remember: Sometimes being a taste berry means walking away.

Taste-berry promise for the day: I will spend my time with friends who are good for me.

327

Everything Works Out for the Best

Love: Don't cry because it is over; smile because it happened.

Vanessa Andrew, 16
Taste Berries for Teens #3

Can you look back on a broken friendship or romance and smile—remembering the fun times? Are you able to look past the heartache of the last days to the laughter of the first ones? Do you see the lessons you learned as something that can help strengthen you and your next relationship? The experience of joy is a choice we make, a mental decision to see reasons to be joyful—and to view them as a valuable solution for any situation—even those of heartache. Choosing joy in this way—choosing a smile rather than tears—is choosing faith: Believing that no matter what, everything is working out for the very best. Ask yourself, "What lessons did the experience bring me? How has it all worked for the good in my life?"

Taste-berry promise for the day: I will journal on a situation that at the time seemed "awful," but in retrospect seems more funny than catastrophic!

Day 329

Know Your True Worth

It's always wise to know yourself before you expect someone else to know you.

Marie Benton, 15
Taste Berries for Teens

Who are you? Do you believe that you are special and valuable? If not, how can you feel as if you have anything to share with others? The truth is that you are valuable beyond measure. But this is something you need to know for yourself, because if you don't believe it, no one else will be able to convince you of it. Even if they act as if you are worthy, you will either not believe them, or you'll be so "needy" and dependent on their praise and validation that soon enough you'll change their minds. Either way, you will stay convinced that who you are is not so cool after all. A far better alternative is to get to know yourself and your true worth: Discover who you are—your likes, dislikes, what you are really good at, how you respond to stressful times and new situations, what you value most and what gives your life meaning. When you truly know yourself, you will know—and believe—that you have so much good to share.

Taste-berry promise for the day: I will tell a friend something he or she doesn't know about me.

Have a Winning Attitude

Success in life isn't a given—it costs attitude, ambition and acceptance.

Jennifer Leigh Youngs
Taste Berries for Teens

As you're probably finding out, a "winning attitude" goes a long way toward being successful. So does believing in yourself and putting your best foot forward. And, of course, so does having goals and a plan to do what it takes to reach them. This can involve hard work, and it almost always requires determination. Success doesn't just happen as if by magic; it usually demands genuine commitment. Along the way, there are sure to be setbacks, sometimes even failures. These times call for acceptance and a decision to pick yourself up, brush yourself off and learn from your stumble on the road to success. Then it's time to keep on moving toward your goals. These are the ambitious attitudes and actions that assure you victory in reaching your goals. Own them and you will know the taste berry of success.

Taste-berry promise for the day: I will talk to my parents about what I've learned from a setback or failure.

Broken Hearts Heal

When your heart gets broken, only one side breaks.

Jennifer Leigh Youngs
Taste Berries for Teens Journal

Has your heart ever been broken? Did you feel like it was completely shattered? Did you feel like you'd never be "okay" again? Even if you thought you were sure to feel that way forever, no doubt you learned this wasn't so—you recovered. While heartbreak teaches us our hearts are fragile, and we can feel as though we are broken right along with them, we also learn, in spite of the way we feel, there's a side of our heart that can never, ever be broken! This lesson is learned as we stand with our heart in our hands, soothing ourselves, nurturing ourselves, loving ourselves. This is encouraging news! You are always there to pick up the pieces of your broken heart and gently put yourself back together. Your love is guaranteed. And so, the truth is that although your heart may get "chipped," it can never be completely broken!

Taste-berry promise for the day: I will write myself a love letter.

Mountains Out of Molehills

I used to stress out so much that I made my problems worse than they were. So now I try not to make mountains out of molehills.

Jamie Dykes, 14
A Taste-Berry Teen's Guide to Managing the Stress and Pressures of Life

Do you sometimes make a problem bigger than it really is? Usually problems, like mountains, are never as daunting as they look. Consider those times when the worst actually did happen: Did you survive it? If you had hoped a special someone was going to ask you to the prom and he (or she) didn't, did you live through not going to the prom with that person? Weeks later, were you on to new worries, new concerns and maybe even a new special someone? Was there ever a time when you were afraid to return a library book because it was long overdue? Did you really get into all that much trouble when you finally did return it? Did your parents stop loving you, or did your friends stop liking you? Probably not. While your worries and fears are real, they are not the end of the world. Don't magnify them in your mind. When you've got a problem staring you down, work toward resolving it. And if things don't turn out the way you planned, know that tomorrow will come anyway. And you will be okay.

Taste-berry promise for the day: I will think of all the ways that I've overcome past problems.

Get On with Life

It doesn't pay to waste time getting down on yourself; it's better to get on with life. Like they say, "Nothing is as far away as a minute ago!"

J. J. Bailey, 17
A Taste-Berry Teen's Guide to Setting & Achieving Goals

Are you down on yourself for losing out on something or having lost time stuck in a rut? Are you disappointed that you got off track or lost sight of your goals? Have you ever been discouraged with a failure and felt as if you might as well just give up on a goal altogether? Certainly you want to be reflective and learn from these experiences, but even so, do not dwell on the past for too long. Each day is an opportunity for a new beginning—and that means today. If you're off course, don't waste your time regretting, finding fault or looking for an excuse. It's not productive to do so, and you'll only end up getting even more down on yourself. Instead, pick yourself up, regroup and get in gear: Review your goals, "reset" your determination to accomplish them and get started again.

Taste-berry promise for the day: I will share all my goals for the day with a friend.

Take Responsibility for Your Actions

I had a habit of always placing blame on others. Then one day, while I was pointing a finger at the other person, I noticed four were pointing back at me! Since then, I've decided to take responsibility for my own actions—which puts me in a more powerful position!

Christopher Brackett, 17
A Teen's Guide to Living Drug-Free

Have you ever chosen to "step up to the plate" and take some truly awesome action to better yourself or someone else? Recognizing our "highest and best" is always gratifying. Have you ever chosen to do something that went against your values or hurt someone else? It can be humbling to see where some of your mistakes have led you. Either way, wise choices or poor ones, you alone are responsible for your actions. Whether a particular decision was yours alone or you were following the crowd, admitting and owning your choices put you in a powerful position. Seeing yourself as responsible for the things you do and say is not only a first step in creating any changes you desire, it also helps you see yourself as maturing. This increases your self-respect, which contributes to your sense of worth. Taking responsibility for the consequences of your actions is what grows the taste berry of self-esteem. See yourself as willing and able to take charge.

Taste-berry promise for the day: I will make a list of all the ways I've taken responsibility for my actions this week.

Stay True to Who You Are

*T*hese days I'm worrying less about being "perfect"
enough to fit into a "bouquet": I'm just working on
being an individual bloom.

Alana Ballen, 13
Taste Berries for Teens

Everyone knows the importance of fitting in and being one of the crowd. It's a normal, healthy desire. But when your focus on fitting in comes at the risk of your physical or emotional well-being, then it is dangerous. What's more, you run the risk of failing to "blossom" to the real truth of who you are. Don't miss out on the opportunity to discover this truth. Ask yourself: "What is most special about me? What are my very best qualities? What traits do I value most about myself? How am I allowing them to have life, to blossom?" Concentrating on yourself as an individual "bloom" benefits not only you, but it also adds to the "whole bouquet." Stay true to who you are. Focus on how you can be a better person—with your own worth being your measure of personal success.

Taste-berry promise for the day: I will look in the mirror and remind myself that my growth as an individual is as important as fitting in with others.

How to Feel Really Human

If you have a chance to do something to help ease the pain of someone, do it. It'll make you feel really human.

Paige Williams, 14
Taste Berries for Teens

Feeling *really human* means embracing your membership in the "human family." Feeling really human means knowing you are sure to feel joy and happiness, as well as being subject to heartbreak and pain. Knowing this you are willing to support others in their joy and in their heartbreak. Feeling really human means recognizing that you are capable of great acts of kindness and feats of strength, as well as of possessing vulnerabilities and weaknesses. Acknowledging this truth about yourself helps you to understand it in others. Therefore, you are better able to inspire them in their greatness and comfort them in their struggles. When was the last time you felt really human?

Taste-berry promise for the day: I will visit someone I know in the hospital.

Like the Way You Look

I *was always stressing-out over having the latest look. If only I'd known then what I know now!*

Jennifer Leigh Youngs
Feeling Great, Looking Hot & Loving Yourself! Health, Fitness and Beauty for Teens

Has a comment on your looks got you scrambling to change them? Do you feel like you'd be totally happy and everyone would want to be your friend if only you looked different than you do? Hopefully, when you look in the mirror to assess your "looks," you are the one who inspires the questions that you ask: "Do I like the way I look? Do I look healthy? Do my eyes and smile show that I'm good-natured and that I like myself? Do I look like a happy person?" It is okay to want to "change" some things about ourselves, but the important thing is to identify what look is *your* best, *your* healthiest—in a word, *you*. Fitting the mold of someone else's ideal is self-defeating. Make sure your own "ideal" is the basis for how you feel about yourself.

Taste-berry promise for the day: I will prepare and eat a really healthy snack.

Evaluate the Trade-Offs

The same snow that covers the ski slopes makes the roads to them impassable.

Bettie B. Youngs
Taste Berries for Teens #3

Have you ever wanted something, not realizing there would be trade-offs to having it? You wanted a part-time job but now that you have one, you've lost the freedom of your time for yourself and your friends on the weekends. You wanted to be a class officer so you could be more popular—and now you have to make unpopular decisions, too. Now that you've finally got your driver's license, your parents will let you use the car on weekends to go out with your friends—but you're also the one who has to pick up your brothers and sisters and take them everywhere. That's the way it is, isn't it? There are trade-offs to most everything—especially things worth having: You have to trudge up the mountain in order to have the thrill of skiing down.

Taste-berry promise for the day: I will make a "pros and cons" list of the trade-offs I'm making in one area of my life—and honestly evaluate if these trade-offs are worth it.

Think About What You Want Out of Life

If you're not thinking about what you want out of life, then you shouldn't complain about not "having a life."

Sarah Knorr, 18
A Taste-Berry Teen's Guide to Setting & Achieving Goals

What is your grandest dream? What is it you aspire to do? What ideals are you striving to uphold? Where do you want to go to college? What kind of career do you want to have? What kind of future do you look forward to creating? Life is filled with so many demands and so much to do, it's easy to just go along for the ride and let the currents take you where they will. However, it's good to know what you want out of life—in the area of grades and education, a career and a future, your social and spiritual life. Identify what you want for today, for tomorrow and beyond. Plan for it and believe you will achieve it. Look in the mirror and you'll see the person in charge of your "having a life"!

Taste-berry promise for the day: I will make an appointment with my school counselor to discuss my plans for my future.

339

Are You a Drama-Mama?

*ry not to be a "Drama-Mama": Such a person is very
taxing to everyone around.*

Jennifer Leigh Youngs
Feeling Great, Looking Hot & Loving Yourself! Health, Fitness and Beauty for Teens

Do you know people who seem to create a lot of drama in their lives? It can be easy to get caught up in that drama—but it's so important to try not to. People who create a lot of drama in their lives often do so for any number of reasons, one being attention. Don't allow yourself to be caught up in someone else's self-productions. Being a taste berry requires that you refuse to co-sign someone else's fabricated disasters—for your sake, as well as theirs. Are you a "Drama-Mama"? Do you take everyday situations and stress and ignite them with emotion and chaos? If so, ask yourself, "What are my motives for doing this? How can I develop *better* and *more effective* skills to cope with people and daily events—stress and all?" Don't earn the reputation of a Drama-Mama! When others see you coming, rather than saying, "Oh, no!" make certain that they're saying, "Oh, yes!"

Taste-berry promise for the day: I will learn and practice a relaxation exercise that works for me.

People Are Priceless

𝒯he most grand and priceless heirloom that my grandmother left is not an outward token, but an imprint etched in my heart of the precious power and grace of her life as a simple and noble person. The legacy she leaves behind is her courageous example of just how pure and simple—and unconditional—her love was.

Jennifer Leigh Youngs
More Taste Berries for Teens

Are there people in your life who are "priceless"? Is it because they inspire you with the way they live their lives daily; their noble goals; the fair and loving ways they treat everyone they know; and that they approach issues and problems in their lives courageously? How lucky for you: Their example shows you the way to do your best and be your best. How awesome to create a living legacy of love, courage and simple nobility. Create this legacy today. Practice the simple daily acts of a true taste berry. Courageously live each day with the power and grace of love.

Taste-berry promise for the day: I will do the laundry or cook a meal for my family.

Pursue Your Dreams Fearlessly

Go after your dreams. Live as fearlessly as you can.

McKenzie Loughlin, 16
More Taste Berries for Teens

Have you ever set out to realize a dream? Didn't having a purpose make you feel as if you were driven with some special brand of enthusiasm? Did you feel fearless in the face of this enthusiasm? When people live wholeheartedly going for their dreams without wavering, it gives them a greater love of life and a better chance of achieving their goals. There is a great freedom that comes with boldly setting out to see your dreams come true. It is the joy of being fueled by a sense of purpose and of knowing that you are choosing to take charge of your life. This wholehearted commitment gives your life deeper meaning and direction and empowers you in a way that keeps you tirelessly on course. Choose to live in this way.

Taste-berry promise for the day: I will create a "dream map" that reminds me of my dreams and inspires me to keep reaching for them.

Seek Comfort in Family

I've learned that uncertain times can cause you to be very certain about the importance of loving your family—and showing it.

Brian Nagle, 15
Taste Berries for Teens #3

Think back on those times when you felt most helpless—whether you were sick, felt enormously downhearted after a certain loss, or were questioning the safety of the world, as so many did on September 11, 2001. Where did you want to go, and who did you want to turn to for help? Chances are, you wanted to go home and seek comfort from your family. When we're feeling most vulnerable, we seek out those who make us feel safe, supported and secure. In such uncertain times, certain members of your family are sure to offer a protective haven to shelter both your body and your heart. Let these people know how much you appreciate them—and show them your love with both your words and your actions. Do all that you can to create daily experiences at home that are powerfully positive and happy.

Taste-berry promise for the day: I will hug every member of my family.

343

Have the Courage to Be "Real"

I've learned the difference between having a "good friend" and having a "close friend": It's about whether or not you're having "real" conversations.

Curt Lindholm, 17
More Taste Berries for Teens

Do you have "friends," "best friends" and "close friends"? Most teens do. What accounts for these differences is the degree to which we are able to be vulnerable and "real." Being "real" is about being able to talk to others at the heart level. This means being able to share an issue or concern that brings up a lot of feelings for you, and having that person sincerely listen without judging, and then the two of you being able to talk things through. It's easy enough to make "small talk" or discuss things going on from the outside, like the weather, clothes, music and the latest gossip at school. It takes a greater level of trust, courage and friendship to talk about what's going on within you: feelings, ideas, beliefs and values. When you talk to your friends at this level, your relationships become more "real," as your ties of honesty, acceptance and trust are deepened. Have the courage to be "real."

Taste-berry promise for the day: I will tell a friend something he or she doesn't know about what I believe in.

Day 345

Give the Gift of Giving

Service gives your life deeper purpose because it creates feelings of connection to others.

Kevin Pauls, 16
Taste Berries for Teens

If you are searching for greater meaning in your life, consider being of service to others. There are many ways to become involved in assisting others—whether it's helping a little brother or sister with homework or sharing part of a holiday to serve a meal in a homeless shelter. If you're wondering how you can make service part of your life, simply take a look around you, or ask your friends, parents, school counselor or your minister. They're sure to know who needs help and what kinds of help they need. Be a taste berry: Give yourself the gift of giving to others.

Taste-berry promise for the day: I will list three ways I would enjoy being of service and make a plan to get involved.

Love Is Inspirational

I'm in love, and it sure brings out the best in me! I'm so much more together and much more motivated: It's not just the weekend I look forward to, but the rest of my life.

Erin Conley, 17
More Taste Berries for Teens

Is there a special someone in your life? Whether there is or it's still a hope for the future, you'll find love changes the way you feel about practically everything! When you're in love, suddenly you are part of something bigger than yourself, and so your life is filled with new meaning and greater hope. You want to give more and be more: You'll find yourself paying more attention to the way you look, as well as to the well-being and happiness of those around you. You'll even notice things you didn't before, such as the many smiles and "hellos" that come your way. You'll smile and say "hi" more easily than ever, too. And you're more likely to feel a greater sense of belonging and want to get involved in community activities. Tapping into the source of love—a universal power—you may notice that you are a part of the entire whole and you'll begin to have an opinion about how others are faring in the world. Love is so inspirational—it helps you see more beauty in life!

Taste-berry promise for the day: I will ask my school counselor about community service opportunities.

"Own Yourself"

espect yourself and be an honorable person. Do all that you can to "own yourself."

Stephen Russell
Taste Berries for Teens #3

How do you "own yourself"? You do so by being honest and authentic, and treating others with respect. In living this way, you are able to put your head on the pillow at night knowing you are right with the world and right with the most important person you spend it with—yourself. When you "own yourself" you consciously take responsibility for what you do and say: Who feels it if you don't eat a balanced diet, get the rest you need or study for the exam? Who feels the satisfaction of being good to another person? Who "stings" the most if you make an inconsiderate remark to someone else? Of course, you are the one who feels these things most. In what ways do you "own yourself"?

Taste-berry promise for the day: I will have a discussion with my friends about all the ways each of us is our own person.

Love Is a Positive Power

Love—feelings and actions motivated by giving and receiving from the heart—is simply an essential ingredient to the well-being of our lives.

Bettie B. Youngs
More Taste Berries for Teens

Love is essential to our health—physically, mentally, emotionally and spiritually. Without it, our lives lack vitality, joy, purpose and meaning. With a good measure of it, we are empowered to live to the fullest. How does being loved make you feel more complete within yourself and more satisfied with life? How does loving others give your life purpose and meaning? Love is simply a positive power in our lives. Always strive to be a loving person.

Taste-berry promise for the day: I will write it upon my heart to be a loving person in all the ways I can.

Learn to "Belong"

Feeling secure, happy and content in our own lives is all about feeling like we "belong."

Larry Epling, 19
More Taste Berries for Teens

We are all journeying in life alongside others—and others are actually vital to our journey. When you have people in your life who love and accept you, people with whom your "place" is assured—you fit in and are a part of them—it helps you feel less alone and lonely as you travel through life. Feeling a part of a whole is the essence of your desire to do good to others, and to make the world safe for everyone who lives in it. It provides you with motivation to be a taste berry. Learn to live in concert and in harmony with those in your world—whether in your family, at school, in your community or the world at large.

Taste-berry promise for the day: I will invite a friend (or my younger brother or sister) to spend time doing something fun with me.

Be a Good Listener

Being a good listener is one of the most important—and ignored—aspects of making and keeping friends, and of getting along with others in general.

Jennifer Leigh Youngs
Taste Berries for Teens

Has there ever been anyone in your life who listened to everything you had to say, serious and light, as if it—and you—truly mattered? Isn't it great to be in the company of these people? Everyone needs to feel valued in this way. Their attention is a sign that they care and that you are worthy of their time. Who makes you feel valued because they genuinely listen as you share your thoughts and feelings? Be a taste berry: Listen attentively to others.

Taste-berry promise for the day: I will be a good listener.

Words Are Powerful:
Use Them Wisely

*O*ur words can hurt—or help—others.

Ellen Abrams, 16
Taste Berries for Teens

Have you ever had your feelings hurt by something someone said? If so, you know the importance of speaking to others with kindness, respect and dignity. Be especially sure that your words aren't mean or insensitive. Even when you say that you're just "calling it as you see it," remember to evaluate your motives. Honesty is a great attribute, but there is a big difference between being honest and being "brutally honest." When considering whether you should speak up and tell someone how you feel, it's good to ask yourself: "Is what I have to say kind? Is it helpful? Is it necessary?" If the answer to any of these is "no," be a taste berry—think of what else you might say that would be kind and helpful. And if you're at a loss for words, heed the instinct: Say nothing.

Taste-berry promise for the day: I will tell a family member or friend everything I appreciate about him or her.

Love Must Be Honest

Love demands complete and total honesty.

Bettie B. Youngs
More Taste Berries for Teens

Does love really have to be honest? Yes, love has to be honest. Has anyone told you that they loved you and the next day showed up holding hands with someone else? Did you "get it" that the love wasn't real? When love isn't honest, it isn't real. When someone else isn't honest with themselves, they can't be honest with you. Likewise, if you aren't being honest with yourself, then you can't be honest with someone else. Are you looking for true love? Are you looking for friendships that are genuinely real? Then you have to be "you" with yourself so that you can be "you" with others. It is only then that the love in any of your relationships is genuine. If you want to have real friends, show them the real you. If you want to have real love, be the real you. If you don't show the real you, how is someone else going to be in love with the real you? Love is a taste berry only when it's honest.

Taste-berry promise for the day: I will be honest with myself and with those I love.

Stand Up for What You Believe

Sticking up for what you believe in shows that you respect yourself.

Chelsey Collinsdale, 15
Taste Berries for Teens

Have you ever seen someone go out of her way to help someone else? What did you say? Hopefully, you told her, "Good for you—that was a really cool thing to do!" Supporting actions of kindness, caring and courtesy shows that you are willing to stick up for the importance of taste-berry values. You may think of "sticking up for what you believe in" as taking a stand against what you believe is wrong, but it is every bit as important to reinforce what you know is right. For example, when someone does something you respect and value, let that person know you appreciate and support her actions. Not only is this a genuine sign of self-respect, but it also gives others permission to do the same. Respect yourself by being true to your beliefs. And praise the admirable actions of others.

Taste-berry promise for the day: I will make a point to praise someone when I see him or her do something I respect.

What Is a True Friend?

All because of one true friend, I learned how to be a friend. As a result, I now have many friends.

Lara Jesiek, 18
Taste Berries for Teens

Do you have a good friend—or many good friends? Does having friends make you feel less alone? Does it make you feel friendlier toward others? What is the value of a friend? A true friend shows you what friendship means, which inspires you to open up to even more of it. A true friend appreciates you in such a way that it gives you more confidence in yourself. A true friend trusts you, so that you have greater trust in others. A true friend is like a seed of grace in your life that plants a harvest of many new friends in your world.

Taste-berry promise for the day: I will let my friends know how much I appreciate their friendship.

Trust Yourself

Trusting yourself is all about having integrity.

Jason Samuels, 16
Taste Berries for Teens

Do you trust yourself to do the right thing, even when faced with tough choices? Do you trust yourself to "get going" when the going gets tough? Do you trust yourself to stick up for yourself and not go along with something you don't want to do? It's difficult to trust others if you don't trust yourself. When you act with integrity, you learn to trust yourself. When you see yourself doing the right thing and measuring your words so that you speak only the truth, then you see yourself as trustworthy. Trust, like integrity, is best learned by experience, which is gained when you consistently see yourself acting in dependable, reliable, honorable ways. On the path of life, you may not be able to trust everybody, but make certain that you know that you can trust yourself.

Taste-berry promise for the day: I will think of three ways that I am trustworthy.

Keep Trying

Hang in there, even when the going gets tough. When you persist, your chances for experiencing success are greater.

Brittany Whiteside, 16
A Taste-Berry Teen's Guide to Setting & Achieving Goals

Has there ever been a time when you didn't manage success with the first try—but were still successful in the end? Maybe you didn't get on the team the first time you tried out but made it the next time. Aren't you glad you didn't give up? We wouldn't get far in life or in reaching many worthy goals if we gave up at the first disappointment (or even at the second or third . . .). In spite of the discouragement you feel over a setback, keep on trying, keep on going, keep on reaching. Even if you feel like your efforts are only accomplishing the smallest degree of progress—progress is progress. As long as you are moving forward, you're still headed in the right direction. "Hang in there" and keep moving forward toward success.

Taste-berry promise for the day: I will hang in there when the going gets tough.

Offer a Sincere Apology

The words, "I'm sorry," have more meaning when you look the person in the eye.

Angie Tyson, 17
Taste Berries for Teens #3

Even knowing that everyone makes mistakes, it's still not always easy to say you're sorry. In fact, it often seems easier to hold your ground and keep on insisting your actions were justified—or to opt for pretending nothing ever happened at all. But a mark of maturity—and of a taste berry—includes both the desire and ability to admit when you're wrong and to willingly take action on "righting" that wrong. This includes offering a sincere apology when you've hurt someone else. Do this by looking the person in the eye, speaking from your heart as you apologize. Why is it so important to look someone in the eye when you say you're sorry? When there's been an argument or hurt feelings, it creates a rift—the connection between you and the other person has been somehow broken, whether a little or a lot. Looking someone in the eye—making true eye contact—connects you to this person. Connecting in this way, each person is able to more readily examine the intent and sincerity of the other person, so trust can be restored.

Taste-berry promise for the day: I will make amends for a wrong for which I am responsible.

Help Others and Feel Good

There is something about helping others that just brings out the best in each of us.

Rhonda Klemmer, 14
Taste Berries for Teens

When was the last time you did something to help someone, and how did it make you feel? Did it make you feel less self-centered? Did it make you feel connected to others? Did it make you feel like a good person? It is a good feeling to help others. And it helps other people feel good, too. Helping others has a self-perpetuating energy: You do something good and so you feel good about yourself. The person you helped feels good about you and about himself that he was worthy of your time and attention. This will motivate him to assist someone else, who in turn will be inspired to help out another person. There's no end to the good that helping others can accomplish as it brings out the best in each of us. Make a point to help someone else today.

Taste-berry promise for the day: I'll assist someone who looks like they could use a hand.

Love Yourself

O ne of the most important things we do in life is learn to love ourselves and others, and to do all things with love.

Bettie B. Youngs
Taste Berries for Teens

What is the most important thing you'll ever do in your life? Get a college education? Better your own life and the life of your family? Discover the cure for cancer or eradicate a disease that plagues mankind? All of these are worthy goals—yet perhaps none of them is more important than learning to love oneself. We always use these words—but do we really know what it means to love oneself? Loving oneself means to think of yourself as a living, breathing human being who needs to be cared for. And taking care of yourself requires that you consider what it takes to keep your body healthy. Loving oneself means doing those things that keep your heart happy and safe—for example, avoiding company with those who are emotionally or physically abusive. Loving oneself can mean everything from honoring that you are a loving person to understanding the source of all love. Once we get clear about all these ways to love ourselves, it makes it easier to love others and to do all things with love.

Taste-berry promise for the day: I will make a list of all the ways I love myself.

Keep a Journal

Putting your thoughts in writing—journalling—is a powerful tool to help you work through your thoughts, feelings and problems.

Melissa Miranda, 18
A Teen's Guide to Living Drug-Free

Have you ever had a rough day and written a letter to a friend airing all the details of what you were going through only to find you felt so much better afterward? Have you written in your diary after a particularly stressful day and discovered you felt like a weight had been lifted from your shoulders just by writing about it? Writing out your feelings, frustrations, angers, fears and hopes can be a great source of relief, as well as a positive way of managing stress. Not only does it let you safely express your feelings, which eases your tension, but getting your thoughts out of your head and down on paper slows you down—which makes it easier to sort things out and look at them objectively. This helps you come to a clearer perspective, so you can find the best possible solutions. Journal regularly. And don't forget to write about all the good in your life, as well.

Taste-berry promise for the day: I will keep a journal.

Day 361

Give and You Shall Receive

T hinking of others is one of the most important things I've ever done for me.

Colleen Morey, 20
More Taste Berries for Teens

Can you remember a time when you've reached out to help someone who was hurting or in trouble? Can you recall the satisfaction you felt in getting outside of yourself in order to reach out to someone else? Any of the petty worries of the day were no doubt forgotten. It's a well-known paradox that when you "lose yourself" to help others, you can actually "find yourself." Giving to others, helping and caring and being of service to them, breathes greater life into the deepest truth about who you are, as it calls you to more love, more compassion, more connection. It reminds you of the essential unity of all humanity and your place as a precious part of its greater whole. Reach out to give, and you'll find you have received.

Taste-berry promise for the day: I will be especially patient and understanding today.

See Truth Through Everyday Eyes

The way to see truth is through your everyday eyes.

Katerina Marie Kothen, 18
Taste Berries for Teens #3

What are your top three truths? Is it being loyal to your best friend? Is it being honest with your parents? Is it being kind to everyone in your world? What does it mean to see these kinds of truths through your everyday eyes? It means seeing them as something you can and should practice daily. To see being loyal to your best friend through your everyday eyes means you don't join in gossip about her with another friend. To see being honest with your parents through everyday eyes means admitting you had friends over when they went out for dinner and asked you not to have company while they were gone. To see being kind to everyone in your world through everyday eyes means holding the door to the school office open for the person who is walking in after you—even if you're in a hurry or the person is not in your circle of friends. The way to see truth through everyday eyes is to see how you can live it right now, today, in all your interactions and relationships.

Taste-berry promise for the day: I will be truthful in everything I say and do.

Someone for Everyone

ℒove ... It comes and goes as it pleases, never failing to make someone happy.

Kayleigh Minutella, 14
More Taste Berries for Teens

Have you watched friends break up who were once so "in love"—only to see each one fall in love with someone else once again? Have you ever been dumped or "really" in love but then fallen out of love? In no time, didn't someone even more "right" for you come along to fill your heart with happiness? Did you learn that while love "comes and goes," there is enough to go around for everyone? It's the way of love! When you take a look around, you'll find love is everywhere. There seems to be someone for everyone. When you're going through a breakup, you may feel as if love has deserted you—but take heart in knowing that it is sure to show up in your life once more—for love is a taste berry that always has its own best interests at heart!

Taste-berry promise for the day: I will talk to a friend about why I believe there's someone for everyone.

Believe in a Greater Power

When you believe in a higher power, your burdens feel lighter, your life is brighter.

Carmen Stork, 16
Taste Berries for Teens #3

Believing in something greater than yourself can bring your life clarity and focus. It can even help everything in your life make sense. If your life is a mess and chaotic, it can help you turn it around. It can bring you peace and calm when you're feeling restless and anxious. When you're feeling uncertain, it can provide stability and direction. It can fill you with a sense of wholeness. If you're feeling sad, it can bring you comfort and even joy. When you're feeling on top of the world, it can take you even higher. Belief allays the bitterness of the hard times and sweetens all the happy times: A sweeter taste berry cannot be found.

Taste-berry promise for the day: I will say a sincere prayer to ask for greater "belief."

You Are a Taste Berry!

It's important to see ourselves in the most positive light that we can. Seeing the good in ourselves helps us to do better, to "be" better.

Bettie B. Youngs
Taste Berries for Teens

Knowing how important it is to see yourself in the most positive possible light, inventory your assets: How are you spectacular? What are your best qualities? What are your greatest successes? How are you a good friend, a good son or daughter, student or grandchild? You are a taste berry. Think about all the ways this shows up in how you treat yourself and others. As you look at all the ways you do good and are good, you are sure to be inspired to act in these ways even more. Follow the lead of this inspiration, and you'll shine in the spotlight of your own good.

Taste-berry promise for the day: I will make a list of all the ways I am a taste berry.

About the Authors

Bettie B. Youngs, Ph.D., Ed.D., is a Pulitzer Prize–nominated author of twenty-six books translated into thirty-one languages. Bettie is a former Teacher of the Year, university professor and consultant to schools nationwide. A long-acknowledged expert on teen issues, Dr. Youngs has frequently appeared on *The Good Morning Show, NBC Nightly News,* CNN, *Oprah* and *Geraldo. USA Today,* the *Washington Post, Redbook, McCall's, U.S. News & World Report, Working Woman, Family Circle, Parents Magazine, Better Homes & Gardens, Woman's Day* and the National Association for Secondary School Principals (NASSP) have all recognized her work. Her acclaimed books include: *Taste Berries for Teens: Inspirational Short Stories and Encouragement on Life, Love, Friendship and Tough Issues; Safeguarding Your Teenager from the Dragons of Life; A Teen's Guide to Living Drug-Free; Helping Your Child Succeed in School; Taste-Berry Tales;* the Pulitzer Prize–nominated *Gifts of the Heart* and the award-winning *Values from the Heartland.* Dr. Youngs is the author of a number of video-cassette programs and is the coauthor of the nationally acclaimed Parents on Board, a video-based training program to help schools and parents work together to increase student achievement.

Jennifer Leigh Youngs is a speaker and workshop presenter for teens and parents nationwide. She is the author of *Feeling Great, Looking Hot & Loving Yourself! Health, Fitness and Beauty for Teens* and coauthor of *Taste Berries for Teens: Inspirational Short Stories and Encouragement on Life, Love, Friendship and Tough Issues; Taste Berries for Teens Journal; More Taste Berries for Teens; A Taste-Berry*

Teen's Guide to Managing the Stress and Pressures of Life; Taste Berries for Teens #3: Inspirational Stories on Life, Love, Friendship and the Face in the Mirror; A Taste-Berry Teen's Guide to Setting & Achieving Goals and *A Teen's Guide to Living Drug-Free.* Jennifer is a former Miss Teen California finalist and Rotary International Goodwill Ambassador and Exchange Scholar. She serves on a number of advisory boards for teens and is a Youth Coordinator for Airline Ambassadors, an international organization affiliated with the United Nations that involves youth in programs to build cross-cultural friendships; escorts children to hospitals for medical care and orphans to new homes; and delivers humanitarian aid to those in need worldwide.

To contact the authors, write to:

Youngs, Youngs & Associates
3060 Racetrack View Drive
Del Mar, CA 92014
or, *www.tasteberriesforteens.com*

More from Bettie
and Jennifer Leigh Youngs

Guides for Life!

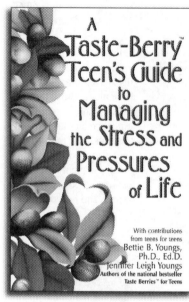

A
Taste-Berry
Teen's Guide
to
Managing
the Stress and
Pressures
of Life

With contributions
from teens for teens
Bettie B. Youngs,
Ph.D., Ed.D.
Jennifer Leigh Youngs
Authors of the national bestseller
Taste Berries™ for Teens

Have you ever had a day when you felt overwhelmed, down-and-out or simply "at wit's end"? On the days when stress sets in, pressures mount and anxiety lingers this book is yours. *A Taste Berry Teen's Guide to Managing the Stress and Pressures of Life* will help you.

Code #9322 • Paperback • $12.95

Want to be more in charge of your life? This book will help you set and achieve goals to shape the direction of your life.

A
Taste-Berry
Teen's Guide
to Setting &
Achieving
GOALS

Bettie B. Youngs, Ph.D., Ed.D.
Jennifer Leigh Youngs
Authors of the bestselling
Taste Berries™ for Teens series and
Feeling Great, Looking Hot & Loving Yourself!

Code #0405 • Paperback • $12.95

Available wherever books are sold.
To order direct: Phone 800.441.5569 • Online www.hci-online.com
Prices do not include shipping and handling. Your response code is BKS.